SHAKESPEARE IN TROUBLE

Chris Cr‹

GW00600593

A Case for Richard Palmer, Investigator

Shakespeare 400: 1616–2016

AESOP Modern
Oxford

AESOP Modern
An imprint of AESOP Publications
Martin Noble Editorial / AESOP
28 Abberbury Road, Oxford OX4 4ES, UK
www.aesopbooks.com

First edition published by AESOP Publications
Copyright (c) 2015 Chris Crowcroft

A catalogue record of this book is
available from the British Library.

First edition 2015

ISBN: 978-1-910301-28-9

Printed and bound in Great Britain by
Lightning Source UK Ltd,
Chapter House, Pitfield, Kiln Farm,
Milton Keynes MK11 3LW

SHAKESPEARE IN TROUBLE

For all who have helped and encouraged.

Note: dates used obey the modern calendar not the old, as is usual historical practice. The opening events are located in February 1601, not 1600 as would have been the case at the time when the year changed after March 25th, not December 31st.

~ 1 ~

I N A CLERKENWELL tenement, harsh morning light was
seeping across a murky room. A rat, carrier of the flea
which infects and kills, hesitated in its darting passage
under the bed in which a man was turning heavily, away
from the dawning light. The rat scuttled on.

Apart from the bed – a solitary family heirloom – Richard
Palmer owned nothing of consequence. Sleep fended off the
daylight gathering over him. A nearby church bell clanked out
an early hour into his dreams, dreams in which people were
running for their lives, ordinary people out walking in sight of a
sluggish-grey river. Tons of galloping horseflesh scattered them.
As if in warning, church bells were rioting all around...

Who were these riders? What were they shouting? Their
voices faded, unanswered. In the dream the pack rumbled on,
acrid foam flecking the horses' hides. Why were they going the
wrong way?

The dream vanished. Palmer turned again in his bed.

Outside it was the first hour of the working day – shutters
opening, folk bustling in the street, gutter slops sharpening the
reek of city life and steaming in the cold February air.
Drinking-houses were opening their doors to early customers,
at the same time throwing out the human leftovers of the night
before. It was a perfectly normal day – for the day after an
armed revolt against the Queen and her Government.

Half asleep, Palmer registered a loud knocking. He woke
abruptly to the sound of a splintering crash as two heavies
kicked open his door. He felt rough hands haul him out of bed.

'Richard Palmer?' the first one demanded. 'Official
business, orders from Chief Minister Cecil.'

Palmer knew better than to argue. He rubbed his eyes.
'There's a name from the past,' he said.

They rode south down Farringdon Street, skirting the old City
walls on their left; Palmer mounted up uncomfortably in front
of the leading rider. He had expected signs of determined
authority. He saw none, only normal traffic for a cold Monday
morning. Had he imagined the events of the day before?
Richard Palmer – former soldier, failed lawyer, ex-everything
including his place in the social order, needed explanations he
knew he would not get, not yet.

They came to Ludgate, western entry to the City. It was
where he had been standing the day before, on his way to his
regular drinking hole in preference to the law's demand, that he
attend church to hear the messages the authorities tuned the
preachers to recite. He had seen them ride by, the riders in his
distorted dream.

'England has been sold out to the Spaniards!' The cry was
taken up by several in the pack.

It was all coming back to him.

They were the bodyguard loyal to Robert Devereux, Earl of
Essex, unstable human gunpowder – why? Palmer knew why.
They'd been cooped up for weeks in the townhouse of their
chief while the Government argued over his fate. More than a
hundred of them, they outnumbered the guards in the Palace of
Whitehall to their west. There Elizabeth was sitting tight after
forty years and more on the throne, refusing to give up power,
refusing to die. Essex had been her favourite but his star had

crashed to earth. Armed force, he must have thought, was his only hope to rise again, or even to survive; and implicate Spain, the evil empire, author of Armada and attempted invasion only a dozen years ago.

So why had the pack headed east away from her?

Essex wanted the backing of the City fathers. That was the word afterwards, in the Bell inn on Carter Lane hard by St Paul's, Palmer's Sunday morning destination and the cause of his hangover today. The City meant money and arms – the Government must surely have known know this, their spies were everywhere. He'd take their shilling himself if it was offered, it was his business these days; he was an informer or, as he preferred to call himself with a nod to his classical education, an *investigator*.

He cast his mind back, piecing together the events of the day before. What had happened to the horsemen after they passed through Ludgate?

A man breathless with the news had turned up in the Bell with the explanation – he'd seen Essex's men arrive at the house of the Sheriff further east on the far side of the City.

'They said they wanted muskets and pistols, as many as the Sheriff had. 'Course 'e said he had to talk to the Lord Mayor first. Silly fools let him go. It was the last they saw of him! Next thing, the Royal herald was riding up with a proclamation against them. I didn't stick around, I can tell you! And they wasn't long after me...'

'Who were they all?'

Palmer's question the day before repeated in his head.

'Essex, his mate young Southampton ... old Blount was there, Essex's father-in-law, likely thought 'e had no choice. There were others too – Lord Monteagle and a couple more of 'is sort...'

Catholic malcontents, Palmer took the man to mean. Some clung to the old faith despite the necessity to subscribe to the new. His own father, now, the holy fool...

'... the Danvers brothers...'

Palmer had snapped back to attention. The Danvers, friends of Southampton, they were always up for trouble.

'... and one of them rash Percys.'

One thing united them. They were all out of favour with the Queen for one reason and another and their unifying hope was Essex. Palmer knew why – Lord Essex had squandered men and, even worse in the Queen's eyes, *treasure* in a failed campaign against the Irish rebels across the sea. He'd abandoned his troops to flee back to London to plead his case to her as to why. No wonder the Government was after his neck! Or that he'd felt he had little to lose. So men out of favour with the world stuck to him like burrs to wool. If he rose again so might they. It was last chances all round.

'Riders coming back,' somebody shouted, relaying a message from out in the street.

Palmer had been first out and along Carter Street to get up to the hill of St Paul's. The band that rode past was diminished – in numbers and in spirit. Essex wasn't leading. His eyes were everywhere, wild, panicked, his lieutenant was driving him forward in the middle of the pack, horse leaning into horse – the young Lord Southampton, Palmer recognised, still determined, still in the game.

His eyes followed the pack galloping west out of the City, to the bottom of the hill where he saw that the gate west was blocked by a company of Government soldiers – newly posted to keep the insurgents in, no question. The front rank held their weapons at the ready, metal glinting dully in the winter air while the other ranks scurried into position behind them. Smart work, the old soldier in Palmer reckoned, and not a moment too soon. Somebody in authority knew what they were doing. The rebels were bottled in.

'Our orders are to bar your way, gentlemen,' the hardened military voice of the Government commander could be heard to bawl out. 'We shan't shoot unless you do.'

A violent lurch of his horse appeared to pitch Essex forward. It pranced nervously within a pike's length of the bristling phalanx blocking the path ahead.

'Shoot!'

The demand from an unidentified voice grew into a chorus. A pistol cracked. An officer among the defenders was falling, in slow time or so it appeared to Palmer from his vantage point.

The Government commander's order cut through the din.

'Musketeers – take aim ... *fire!*'

Palmer had heard the order and instinctively stepped back – his days of walking towards the sound of guns were long over. He saw before he heard the ferocious volley which blazed out from the defenders' weapons, long barrels against short. In the chaos of rucking beasts and cursing human voices, a boy – a page? – slumped out of the saddle down among a terrified tattoo of trampling, mangling hooves. Civilian bystanders were running to the aid of two of their number mown down in the crossfire, the screams from their writhing bodies piercing the broil.

A counter-charge by the insurgents drove in among the pikemen, swords clanging against metal and wood in desperate attempts to beat down the thrusting pikes. An old man among the rebels – Blount? – took a practised pikejab in the face. He fell from his horse, spitting blood and teeth from the look of it – old men and boys, they had no business here to Palmer's mind.

The attack had recoiled like sea from the shore. It drew the pikemen on in a slow, disciplined advance, boots crunching in time on the roadway, pikes extended resolutely in front of them.

'Retreat!' a voice hollered among the horsemen.

Even fewer horses began to career back uphill. Before they reached Palmer they swung south towards the river, maybe a third of the force first seen piling into the City.

He watched them go then followed in their wake once he saw that the Government men were holding their position, not pursuing.

He saw a group of Londoners lift chains closing off the escape route to let the rebels through. Sympathy or just a desire to get rid of them? The result was the same. Palmer followed them at a distance down towards the riverside.

At the water's edge the riders abandoned their horses.

'It's a mistake going back west,' an unidentified voice protested. 'We should strike out east, pick up a boat for France.'

Palmer had spied from a doorway – as little as a day, as much as a life before – as Essex stood up to his full height, elongated by his high-crowned hat which was punctured by bullet holes.

'I am not running away, I am not a traitor. It's the Government who will have to answer for this. We still have the hostages in Essex House.'

''Ere, oo's goin' to pay?' a startled waterman protested as armed men hurtled past him into his ferry, one of several Southampton was busily commandeering.

'Just shut up and row!' Southampton snarled.

The waterman was not the only man put out of sorts. A late rush from some laggards among the insurgents caught up with Palmer as he emerged from the doorway and bundled him on board.

'Don't want any nosey parkers lurkin' round here, do we?' his captor said, a little fighting cock of a man, Welsh by the sound of him.

Looking down the barrel of a horse pistol, Palmer had decided not to argue.

The passage on the river had been like the calm after a storm. Punting west upstream, no boats came in pursuit.

'I shouldn't be here,' Palmer complained.

His captor gave him a disdainful look. It directed him to the water.

Swimming in the ice-cold Thames in winter? Not the best plan, Palmer decided.

At the river stairs by the rear of Essex House, the survivors disembarked. Palmer made himself scarce in a corner of the courtyard. News given to the insurgents appeared to dispirit them even more. The guards holding the hostages had panicked.

'We reckoned it best to let the hostages go.'

It was a day for bad timing.

'... and Government troops have the place surrounded.'

Essex looked more lost than ever.

'What do we do now?' he begged Southampton, overheard by everyone in the yard including Palmer who had pulled the brim of his hat down as far as he could.

'Burn papers, anything that might incriminate us!'

There were women in the way, Essex's sister for one, once the idol of a fashionable poet.

'What will we do, Henry?' she pleaded to Southampton.

A cry of warning gave the answer.

'They're attacking the front gate!'

'We fight!' Southampton insisted, pushing her aside.

Palmer was given no choice but to join the body of men following him. His captor thrust the handle of the horse pistol towards him. Palmer refused it – he was in enough trouble as it was.

'No fight in your belly, is it?' his captor sneered.

The Government assault came on in force, companies of infantry backed by cavalry with artillery behind them, a giant hammer to crack a shrivelling nut – the powers-that-be were taking no chances. Fierce shouts of men getting into battle rage shattered the frigid air. Concerted gunfire rang out – the defenders putting up a resistance. Palmer kept his head down and followed the old soldier's maxim – never volunteer. He stayed unarmed.

He saw two attackers fall, only for more to pile over them regardless, overwhelming the gates. They flooded into the courtyard. Wreaths of pungent gunsmoke thickened the mist of the shortening winter afternoon.

The defenders fell back into the main building, taking Palmer with them.

A window shattered. Palmer's captor crumpled, hitting the ground senseless as blood began to seep from his chest, his feet beating a dying rhythm on the wooden floor. The women screamed. Palmer edged further out of the way.

'Be quiet for God's sake,' Southampton yelled.

Another defender span across the room among shards of leaded glass, shot down in the same way. The women's screaming turned epic.

'Get them out of here!' Southampton ordered men around him. 'Block the windows, use anything you can find, books from the library, anything...'

He led by example. A slim book of poetry fell open as he grabbed it. He flung it aside as thin and useless, in Palmer's direction who caught it.

'Right Honourable, I know not how I shall offend...'

the words in front of him read. He was in the middle of a battle and like as not to get himself killed, and here he was reading a fawning dedication by some poxy poet! God how he hated modern poetry!

Something had changed. What? Why the silence? The firing had stopped. The quiet was unnatural. A voice from the Government side called out.

'We are prepared to offer you terms for surrender.'

Palmer looked around. Essex was sitting on a chair in a corner bent into himself, rocking away in a world of unfeelingness. But Southampton was busy stumbling over the two dead men, the smell of their blood and the shit from their death-loosened bowels tainting Palmer's nostrils for the first time. Where was he going? Up the stairs onto the roof.

'We will only explain our actions to the Queen in person,' Palmer next heard him call out from somewhere above, in a voice at breaking point, unused to battle commands. 'And you must give us hostages to ensure our safe return.'

The Government commander was having none of it.

'My Lord Southampton, subjects do not bargain with princes. This building cannot possibly withstand artillery fire, which we *will* use.'

Shit! Artillery! Palmer's reaction was like a cornered rat searching for a safe hole. A ridiculous line in Latin kept running through his mind uninvited, that mice never trust to one hole alone. Where could he run?

'Then we would rather die like *men*, with swords in our hands,' he heard Southampton shout.

'Yes, yes, like men!'

A different voice was shrieking and cursing from somewhere on the roof as well. It was Essex's, out of control. When in God's name did he get up there?

'We must have a truce,' Southampton called down. 'There are women inside.'

And me, Palmer wanted to say. Never mind the women, what about me? I shouldn't be here, I'm nothing to do with this lot...

He heard the truce agreed and saw the women evacuated. He listened to the few defenders left wrangle over their position. Southampton stood up in disgust.

'It's finished.'

He started to walk out, towards the lines of the Queen's troops.

'The old bitch can't live for ever,' Southampton muttered angrily as he went.

Palmer didn't go with him. It was not the first time he'd ever had to make a run for it, in war or peace. He followed his nose, away from the action, down stairs, through a trapdoor into a vault which – glory be! – opened out to the shoreline of the river among the wooden piles of a jetty.

He'd had a muddy time of it picking his way along until he found an old abandoned skiff. It barely got him clear of the area, going with the tide. Clambering ashore, what he had needed more than anything else, that Sunday night, was drink, by a warm fire, back at the Bell.

~ 2 ~

A S PALMER and his escort approached the entrance to the Palace of Whitehall on the morning after the day before, not so far away, by the Long Ditch in St James's, the street rattled with rumours of the previous day's events.

A dark woman listened to each and every one. She was shielding an infant boy, not the son of the husband who beat her for what he'd known when he married her. Him she hadn't seen for a day and a night. He'd left at dawn, out of keeping with the customs of a solemn Sunday.

Something she overheard made Emilia Lanier start.

'They say it's as much Lord Southampton's doing.'

That name. She drew the child closer.

A hundred miles away in the middle of the kingdom, wintry rain was falling over a bleak, colourless landscape. A man was riding doggedly, on the last leg of a journey by night and day. He whispered encouragement into the cocked ears flicking lightly in front of him, his third mount of the forced ride.

Word had come to William Shakespeare in London, warning of what was boiling over in Essex House. It was the signal to run while the eyes of the authorities were busy elsewhere. He had cleared his Bankside lodgings of money, and papers best not left behind.

Caked grey with mud, exhausted, he saw the entrance to the long stone bridge over the river, announcing he was home. The sight of Stratford had never been so welcome or its promise so mired in doubt.

Robert Cecil, Chief Minister looked up at Palmer from his Whitehall desk crowded with papers.

This name from the past was very much there in the present, older, but if anything even more physically insignificant. Palmer watched for some show of recognition, but the man gave him none. Why should there be? Cecil was the most powerful individual in the kingdom after the monarch. Even in their old student days there had been a gulf between them, the one a wealthy student, the other a charity case obliged to serve his betters. Did he think that Robert Cecil's crooked back had ever levelled fortunes between them? It was foolish if he had. He tried to ignore his own shabbiness now.

'I hope my men were not rough,' Cecil said.

The straight answer should have been yes. Palmer was tempted to say it too, thinking of his rude awakening and the hurried horseback journey mounted up in front like a prisoner.

He bowed politely instead.

'I have an important assignment for someone of your ... trade,' Cecil said. 'It is to do with yesterday's trouble with Lord Essex.'

Palmer put up an alert, expectant expression – he needed the work, he needed the money and above all, he must keep quiet about getting mixed up in the last stand at Essex House. He brushed aside the unspoken question in his head, why him?

'The Earl of Southampton, what do you know about him?'
Cecil asked.

All lace and no substance, he was tempted to say about the
noble lord but didn't – you could never be sure who was related
to whom. He adopted a professional tone, ignoring his
memories of the day before.

'Catholic family, father died when the present Earl was an
infant, educated at, um, our college, St John's, Cambridge.'

He glanced across at the Chief Minister for a sign of
recognition of old times shared. None came.

'After that, the usual year at Gray's Inn, studying Law…'

Rich boys having a good time around town. Cecil had,
Palmer hadn't.

'… served under Essex against the Spaniards in the Azores,
and in Ireland last year.'

Palmer took a risk.

'… never fully established himself at court, dependent, too
dependent some say, on Lord Essex.'

Essex's agitated screams on the roof reverberated in his
head. Was that only yesterday?

'That is about the sum of it,' Cecil agreed.

So what did Cecil want? As far as Palmer knew
Southampton was safely locked up with Essex in the Tower,
somewhere he might have ended up himself. He coughed
politely, awaiting instructions.

'How well do you know the playhouses?'

The playhouses? Palmer bit back an honest answer, that he
couldn't stand them. He only went when his work required it –
stinking, squalid places they were, and as for the new drama
performed there! It was devoid of the most basic classical
principles; as one might expect of the uneducated hacks who
wrote it.

'Only in connection with my business,' he replied carefully.

Cecil appeared to be reassured by the answer. He laid out the case.

'The day before yesterday, at the Globe playhouse on Bankside, an old play was resurrected at the special request of the insurgents. They intended to get the mob in the mood for regicide.'

A suspect play? This was news to Palmer; there had been no talk of it in the Bell. He had no idea which play it could be, he was not a follower.

'Richard II,' Cecil said.

The royal name was enough for Palmer. It was infamous, a ruling monarch deposed in favour of a popular rival causing war between the powerful houses of Lancaster and York; and a generation of national misery until the Queen's grandfather – even more of a usurper himself, a jumped-up Welshman! – had settled the realm down by force of arms and taken the throne. We're all Tudors now, he reminded himself in case he spoke out of turn.

'I have a report for you to look at,' Cecil said, referring to the document in front of him. 'Do you know anything about one William Shakespeare? He wrote the play.'

A common sort of name for a common type of character, Palmer reckoned. If he was a player then he was like as not a bad sort, one of the quarrelling, whoring, drinking sort usually pursued by angry husbands and fathers with trouble all round. Good for his business all the same.

'No more than the next man,' he said with a hint of distaste.

Cecil's satisfaction visibly increased. Palmer could guess why. These new plays and their players were a troublesome phenomenon to control – Puritan preachers fulminating against them, the City fathers constantly at the Government to close their playhouses down while the Queen, who liked a play, turned a deaf ear to all of them ... until now, until this Richard play?

Palmer put in a question of his own.

'Isn't this an official matter? Why do you need me?'

Keep your mouth shut, his empty purse complained. Get out of here and stay as far away as you can, his instinct for survival urged.

Cecil toyed with papers in front of him.

'I have learned that it pays to be in possession of all the facts however awkward they may be. Our agents have a tendency to report what travels best, what is *convenient* when they are under pressure. They do their job as they think I want it done. I need an independent investigation, reporting to me alone.'

Palmer understood. There were factions in the Government, he guessed, differing interests rubbing against each other in these awkward times. He was to be a useful pawn in a larger game. He couldn't care less – what clients did with his report was a matter for them.

'Her Highness is especially outraged by the Richard play,' Cecil said. 'Even today, we do not permit it to be published or played with that scene, the er ... deposition of her unfortunate ancestor. 'Do you not know that I am Richard?' That is what she is going round saying. My colleague the Lord Chamberlain has tried to calm her royal displeasure but then, Lord Hunsdon *is* the patron of the offending acting company...'

'So the question is—' Palmer started to say.

The Chief Minister finished his words for him.

'Was Southampton in any way involved in putting the players up to the Richard play?'

Why Southampton, Palmer asked himself? Surely your man would have been Essex or one of his minions. What was interesting Cecil about Southampton?

Cecil pushed over a purse which bulged with coin of the realm, silver at the least Palmer hoped. He also pushed over a satchel.

'It contains the background report I told you about and some other items which should interest you. Take them out and see.'

Palmer covered his surprise at what came out – three slim volumes, the first, he quickly checked, dedicated to Southampton.

'Right Honourable, I know not how I shall offend...'

Where had he seen that before? Oh yes, in the library in Essex House. Say nothing, Palmer.

He shuddered all the same, shutting the book in case it told tales on him. He would read it later over a beer or two purchased with his newfound wealth – when he was safe and sound and far away from Whitehall. His taste buds pricked at the thought.

Feeling Cecil's eyes on him, he delved deeper into the satchel, pulling out a sheaf of papers. On them were handwritten poems, sonnets his eyes quickly told him from their verse form, one per linen sheet which was unusual. Copies for presentation? Fancy goods all the same.

He glanced at the first one. He winced. Palmer hated modern poetry as much as he hated the new drama. He raised an eyebrow towards Cecil.

'We believe they were written by Shakespeare,' Cecil said, 'to Southampton, we presume, since they were picked up last night when our people searched the Earl's house here in town. We think that there may be more.'

More sonnets, Palmer thought, shaking his head.

'... if there are, we should like to see them.'

Sonnet-collecting? Well, there were worse things to be paid for.

'I assume the writer has the full set,' Palmer said.

'Yes, we thought so too. But Mr Shakespeare has disappeared from his lodgings. Nothing of consequence was found.'

'So he's left town? When?'

'A matter of hours.'

Not a man confident of his innocence, Palmer decided; or of innocence being believed.

'... our people are on the lookout in London but they report no sign so far.'

'Anywhere obvious he would run to?'

'We know him to be a Warwickshire man. He keeps up a strong connection with his home town there, Stratford.'

'Stratford? Is that in the brief?' Palmer asked who was lazy about travel. London was his patch.

'If need be. The trial of Lords Essex and Southampton will be Thursday week which gives you ten days. Time is of the essence. What you find could have an important bearing.'

... not on the result of the trial for Essex, both men understood.

'Why is Southampton's case so important?' Palmer heard himself ask.

It was no business of his, normally he just took instructions.

Cecil paused before answering.

'We are in a time of ... uncertainty,' he said, choosing the word with care.

Palmer realised at once what he meant and would not say outright – the Queen was old, nearing her three-score-and-ten. She was unmarried, childless, she had named no heir – it was treason even to talk about it, in private or in public; even to think it – there were plenty of Government lawyers who held that to think was to act; ridiculous, but effective in stifling speculation, at least among the common sort.

But not among the powers-that-be.

Who was Cecil backing, he wondered, in the great succession bet? King James of Scotland, Protestant son of the Catholic mother Mary, the one Elizabeth had executed? Or one of the Spanish mob, more Catholic than the Pope? After the events of the previous day, it certainly wasn't the Earl of Essex.

'... in a time of uncertainty one seeks to unite the ruling class, not divide them,' he heard Cecil explain.

Meaning divide as few as possible of them from their heads?

'... so this is a matter of the greatest importance, Dick.'

Palmer smiled inwardly at the politician's trick of personalisation. He got to his feet. Cecil appeared unwilling to let him go. Had he something more to add?

'I shall not ask you what you were doing among the rebels yesterday...' Cecil began to say.

Palmer turned cold. Of course, the Government would have had men among the rebels, but men who knew him? His captor? The man was dead. Dead men told no tales...

'... as much as we know what you are – an informer – we also know that you have no history with Lord Essex and his ilk. Perhaps you were on business for someone else?'

Agree with him, just lie, Palmer told himself. But he heard himself telling the truth.

'No, I was curious, I got too close and was swept up in it. It was better not to argue. As you say, I'm not one for getting mixed up in politics as a rule...'

Cecil looked at him for several seconds before speaking.

'I believe you. In fact it helped me make my decision...'

'That I saw some of the suspects close to?'

'Yes, that ... and that what we know, and have in evidence is, shall we say, helpful in encouraging your utmost efforts?'

So Cecil had something on him – it was the Government's regular way with its informers. Palmer bowed his way out with the satchel – any further familiarity on his part would not be right; the order of things had changed, they were master and servant now.

The man who escorted him out of Cecil's chamber introduced himself as Cecil's chief official. They walked together through the gaudily painted brickwork of the Palace enclave towards Whitehall stairs, the jumping off point for river transport which was the quickest way around the capital.

'We know your work, Mr Palmer,' the man said to him.

It took Palmer a second or two of blood-pulsing alarm before he decided that his part in the events of the day before was not what the man was alluding to.

'I knew your father,' the man added, more significantly.

So that was it.

Palmer turned towards the official. He was elderly and monkish in appearance. Was he? Some in the Queen's service still were, among her courtiers and servants. It was said that she asked no questions, made no windows into men's souls as she put it if they were loyal to her, swore the oath of allegiance and did their job. A man might mouth the new rite while privately rehearsing the prayers of the old.

So this old official was a friend of his father. A friend of a holy fool more like! Palmer wanted nothing to do with reminiscences of a past he preferred to forget, a past full of struggle and loss over slivers of difference in quarrelling faiths otherwise alike as twins. It was why he was where he was now, doing other men's bidding rather than enjoying the family estate in Kent. The old Palmer lands were in other hands now, thanks to the foibles of his father.

He said nothing more but hailed a waterman to take him east towards the City without looking back. He disembarked on the Blackfriars side short of London Bridge. He found Ave Maria Lane – old name despite the new religion. Within sight of St Paul's Cathedral, he entered the Stationers Hall, home of the regulators of the publishing trade.

He checked the records until he found what he was looking for – The Life and Death of King Richard the Second. He found out which bookseller stocked the play in St Paul's Churchyard nearby. This was not to be his immediate destination. He retraced his footsteps back to Carter Lane. He went into the Bell inn.

Time to drink and think, he promised himself.

~ 3 ~

SUSANNA SHAKESPEARE, elder daughter of her house in Stratford, got no explanation when the mud-pasted figure of her father appeared, out of the rain and into the house in front of her. He was distracted in his greeting, saying little. She watched him strip off his boots then shut himself away in his room, the one in which he habitually slept alone whenever he came home. He didn't even call for warm water. She relayed his orders to the servants that he was not to be disturbed. Listening at the door, she overheard the chest inside being unlocked, the one in which her father stored documents of importance to the family.

Whatever could it mean? Nothing good.

She gave him some time and then she went in with as much hustle and bustle as she could on the excuse of making up a fire in the room. As she did her work, she saw out of the corner of an eye that her father was shivering, even as he was standing by the surging flames. From the papers clutched in his hands and the abstracted look in his eyes, she tried to understand what was going on – she had never seen him like this before.

'Father...'

The prospect of her close to hand seemed to disturb him. She was no longer a child, Susanna reminded herself, she was coming on eighteen, already marriageable. She took pride in being the fruit of his youth, his image in female form, so unlike her mother – her younger sister Judith took after her. Her mother ... a ghost in the house ever since...

Susanna pushed the memory of the golden boy aside. Dead, her brother was, dead, dead these five, six years. She stopped working for a moment to try to remember his face. It

27

wouldn't come. She must concentrate on the living, on the needs of her father. She'd always had a special bond with him.

But shouldn't he honour it as much as she did?

Nothing came from him, just more shivering and the look of a man interrupted, waiting for her to go. His silence nourished her suspicion – her father's surprise return must be due to bad news in London, the place she had never seen except in her imagination, fuelled by her father's stories. Maybe there was plague in the capital and the actors had broken up? It had happened before. Even when it did, he had never been like this before.

She saw herself dismissed by a wave of his hand.

'It's not a good sign,' her grandmother Mary said when Susanna went over to the old family home on the other side of town to give her the news of the strange return and her father's close-mouthed behaviour. 'His father was the same, yow must know, when the last bad times came.'

Times worse than now? As far as Susanna was concerned, life wasn't easy as it was, what with her father away for most of the year except for a midsummer month or two. She couldn't remember when this wasn't how it was. No, it wasn't easy. Her mother's illness, a kind of sad, moping sickness was a lot for a daughter to bear, having to manage the household in her place, denying herself the dreams of the young. Some of her friends were married with children, others had sweethearts or hopes for one. All she had to look forward to was her father coming home with his tales of the big city and the promise that one day, soon, her time would come. But now, would it ever?

She returned home to push again at her father's door with the stubbornness her mother used to chide her over, in her better days – 'yow get it from the Shakespeare side.'

Her father seemed to read her mind.

'You're not to worry, Susanna,' was all he would say to her in an accent marked by the south.

'Mother,' she said instead, 'she's asking after yow.'

'Now is not the time!'

The colour rose in her face. He appeared to ignore it.

'I will see her, when I am ready, soon, only, not now.'

It was two more hours before he kept his word.

Anne Shakespeare was sitting by the kitchen fire, still and silent, distracted by the flames. Even when her husband came up behind her, she gave no reaction. Susanna stayed where she was, unnoticed by either of them, standing at the door, watching.

It was their first meeting since the previous summer, the pattern of the marriage. What was so unusual about that, Susanna's grandmother often said? Plenty of other men went away just as often – at sea, on business, under arms. It was a matter of making a living and getting on in the world. The big house didn't come cheap – the house Susanna's mother didn't like. And where would they all be if he didn't go away to work? Crammed into the old family home with the ageing grandparents and the lummocking, wifeless uncles and a frantic aunt busy raising a late family of her own.

Oh yes, grandfather John liked to reminisce about the glory days when he ran Stratford, arguing with the powers-that-be, fighting for the town's interests up and down the land. For years, the cunning in the old man's head and the fire in his belly had worked until time and circumstance found him out, so grandmother Mary said. Then his name and what he had done meant nothing, they were past deeds, counting for no-thing in a new-thing world.

Money made the difference, *money* talked old Mary liked
to say, and her son had to go to London to get it. He was good
at making it, so grandmother said without knowing how,
sensible in holding onto it – unlike her husband John who'd
played lender and a borrower until each end crushed him in the
middle, so grandmother Mary said.

Susanna watched her father's hand reach towards her
mother's ashen hair. Her mother missed the old place, Susanna
understood, the crowding in of bodies and smells and the
endless drudgery of cooking and cleaning. She missed it as
much as her father couldn't abide it. It was what women did.
Was her mother ever as young as she was now, the daughter
wondered, knowing little of a courting in midsummer fields
making a bed for nature's way and a baby begot out of wedlock,
defiantly baptised with a biblical name for falsely accused
beauty and virtue, Susanna?

Her mother looked round at her father, face reddened by
the heat. Unusually, she spoke first.

'Yow never come near me now.'

Susanna blushed from her vantage point. Not since her
brother died, she knew, and they moved into the big house and
her father took his separate room and left the marital bed.

Her father said nothing in reply.

He had been away when her brother died. The loss wasn't
any fault of her mother's. Children die, so grandmother Mary
said who in the same breath thanked God she'd only lost three
so what was one to Anne? Her son and the family heir, that was
what, as Susanna knew only too well. Where was her father at
the time? On tour, called back to home too late. Too late, what's
more to attend the funeral rites which held no masses in memory
of the dead; or so grandmother Mary said who had no liking for
the new religion and what it had forbidden from the old.

'God knows where the poor lad's soul is now,' the old woman said time after time.

In the London late afternoon, Emilia Lanier heard her husband return.

'Don't ask me where I've been,' he warned her.

'How did you escape?'

His mouth gaped open.

'I don't know what you mean...'

She gave him a hard look.

'All right, all right, I was Essex's man, God damn him, he gave me my officer's commission, I *had* to go with him.'

He eased himself down onto a stool in front of a meagre fire which fluttered rather than blazed.

'That doesn't matter any more. What does,' she continued carefully, 'is that the ... business failed.'

He thrust his head into his hands.

'I know, I know, it was a shambles. When I saw the way it was going, I slipped away so I didn't end up with the other poor bastards, behind bars, or worse – give me credit for that at least.'

She looked him over with barely concealed disgust. He'd consumed her dowry, her jewels and her better years. He had taken but he could not provide.

'We have to think carefully,' she told her husband.

In the back room of the Bell Palmer was relaxing in the warmth of a coal fire, contemplating his pot of beer. Reluctantly, one by one, he pulled out of the satchel the documents given to him by Cecil. He began to read.

The file was a model of its kind, written in the meticulous script, the old-fashioned, stubby secretary hand of Cecil's chief official, bearing today's date, February 9th 1601. It reminded Palmer uncomfortably of his father's. Were the pair at school together, educated by that lost race of monks? He put the thought from his mind as he always did when it turned to memories of his father. He gulped down a draught of beer in preparation for what he was about to read.

William Shakespeare was...

'... a Warwickshire man of ordinary class ... actor and writer, shareholder in the Globe theatre owned by the Lord Chamberlain's Men ... money from writing, acting fees and a share in the playhouse profits ... coat of arms granted and the status of gentleman, motto *Non Sancz Droit.*'

'*Not without Right,*' Palmer translated out loud, 'or took a lot of time, trouble and money!'

He wasn't surprised. The College of Arms was none too scrupulous these days about the claims of those prepared to pay through the nose. He read on.

'Came to London around Armada year ... law case over disputed inheritance (source, Chancery master William Lambarde).'

Lambarde! Well, well, Palmer chuckled, there was a name he knew, his old law tutor in the days when Palmer was going to remake the family fortunes from pleading others out of theirs. So Lambarde was in the know about Shakespeare. Worth going to see him. Old Lambarde, still alive, well well. Dried fruit lasted longest after all.

'Lodged with fellow Stratford man, Richard Field, printer, respectable business, clean file, publisher of Shakespeare's first poetry – *Venus & Adonis*, and *Rape of Lucrece*, '93 and '94 respectively.'

Ah, here it was.

'Both dedicated to Henry Wriothesley, Earl of Southampton.'

Pronounced Ryosely, Palmer reminded himself and then laughed – it had been Risley once upon a time by all accounts, when the Risleys were attorneys and so no better – in point of fact a darned sight worse – than the Palmers who had lived off their lands for centuries, until...

He wiped the fact from his mind. He took another mouthful of beer before returning to the file.

'Well established by '94. Lists of companies, playhouses, publications and known places of residence (and taxes unpaid) follow.'

Palmer looked them over. The man got around, busy-busy, three plays a year, histories, comedies, romances, moving round the town to follow the work and keep ahead of the taxman!

'Master of the Revels estimates earnings equivalent to a successful lawyer.'

Another Risley on the rise? Or what lawyer Palmer might have achieved? Big money for a Warwickshire man of 'ordinary class'.

'Rumours of a series of sonnets.'

Palmer groaned. Another swig of beer helped him on.

'... privately circulated, but *vide* book of collected poems, several marked which may be his similar to examples found with Lord Southampton after the insurrection by Lord Essex.'

Full marks for having the file up to date!

A plainer voice interrupted him.

'How's Dick then?'

The landlord of the Bell was drawing up a stool and settling himself opposite. For a man who had no friends, he was the nearest Palmer had to one.

'Anything interestin'?' the landlord asked.

'A government job,' Palmer said.

'Better stop waterin' the beer here then.'

Both men laughed – Palmer didn't drink in establishments where the beer was under-strength.

'May take me to Stratford.'

'By Bow?'

'No, upon Avon, Warwickshire.'

The landlord was one of those who liked to be helpful.

'I get a couple of reg'lars in here,' he said, 'well I say reg'lars, see 'em most weeks – a pair of carriers from Stratford, father and son ... Greenaway's the name. If you're looking for safe passage they usually takes a party of travellers back with 'em ... what with the risks of robbers an' that on the road.'

'Could be useful,' Palmer said.

'They usually arrives of a Tuesday. Tomorrow as it happens.'

Left alone, Palmer turned back to his papers. He began to toy with the sheaf of sonnets from the satchel. He read the first line of the top sheet:

'From fairest creatures, we desire increase.'

Not today we don't, he decided, shoving the papers back impatiently. He turned instead to the two other books and their opening words of dedication.

'Right Honourable, I know not how I shall offend...'

The smoke of gunfire infused his memory and the sight of the dead and dying.

'... but if the first heir of my invention prove deformed, I shall be sorry it had so noble a godfather.'

Standard arselicking stuff, he judged, setting it aside before it got to the hated verse.

The equivalent in the second book stopped him in his tracks.

'The love I dedicate is without end. What I have done is yours; what I have to do is yours.'

He rocked back, struck by the change. Published a year apart, the second one in '94 he recalled from the file – not the words of someone about to part ways.

Palmer looked away into the fire in front of him. What did he have so far? Grovelling poet linked with troublesome, rebel lord some time in the past. Strongly enough to commit treason seven years on? A lot could happen in that time. It had for him, from fugitive escaping the learning of law, to soldier in the field, to struggler in the streets of London.

He picked up his pot, only to find it empty. He toyed with the thought of more beer, feeling for the purse safely pocketed inside his clothes. He pulled out one of its coins, holding it up to the light. The Queen's shilling. There was no mistaking the sharp-faced profile – most people knew no other. But the people's love was fading. She was old. Time was when people thought they would live and die under her, but now, this same world was waiting for her to die. She had outlived her age.

He looked at the coin a second time, its silver face glittering in the firelight. This time it was a Government shilling, money from the hard-faced Chief Minister who intended to survive and prosper, who demanded results. He was the future and she was the past. So this was an assignment Palmer had to complete, for good money which would have to be earned.

With a sigh he put down the empty beer mug and made ready to go.

'It's best you disappear for a while, lay low in the country out of harm's way,' Emilia Lanier said, packing her husband off with a show of wifely concern.

He gave her a disbelieving look. He obeyed her just the same. Her spirits rose once she saw that he was gone.

She had not told him of her plans.

Their servant-girl was to look after her boy when she brought him back from school. A journey across town, on foot since she hadn't a penny to waste, and alone, carried risks, after dark many times more. There was a future to be looked into, an astrologer to consult.

She had neither the time nor the money for fear.

~ 4 ~

PALMER WAS SURPRISED to see so much bustle around the Cathedral churchyard after the violent events of the weekend – life was going on all the same.

He watched serving men and women circulating, on business or looking for employment, reading, if they could – or found someone who would – the notices pinned to the Cathedral doors. Tourists stood gawping at the sights and chattering in strange languages – at the men of fashion dressed like embroidered peacocks, preening themselves with nothing better to do while the commoner sort hurried past them on business in their sober black. In the background dealers, prostitutes, conmen and worse milled themselves up into the scene. The smell of food, baked, roasted or over-boiled wafted out from taverns and eating houses.

Palmer's eyes shifted, looking for just one of the many bookstalls for which the churchyard was noted. He made his way to the one he wanted which traded under the sign of the White Greyhound. An unfriendly type was standing out in front, the sort who despised customers. The bookseller's beady eye challenged Palmer not to waste his time, to buy or go.

'A play, by William Shakespeare,' Palmer announced.

The vendor's features formed a sneer.

'Any idea which one?'

'Tell me what you've got.'

The bookseller began to recite his stock in a sing-song voice.

'Histories, comedies and tragedies. King Harries, any number of them – the Sixth, that's in three books, the Fourth which is in two – that's the one with fat Jack Falstaff who

amuses a certain *sort* of client; and the Fifth of course, once
more into the breach dear friends, an' all that. One King John,
but then again, we only ever 'ad one.'

Palmer gave the man no help.

'Comedies then? Well, there's the Errors play, the Shrew –
not much call among the womenfolk for that one and the
married men don't like getting caught with it. No? Love's
Labours, the Merchant, Much Ado. Are we getting closer, *sir*?'

Palmer shook his head.

'I'll know it when you say it,' he promised.

'Tragedy then – and this is my last shot. Now let me see, oh
yes, how about his Romeo, a real tearjerker with the ladies, or
... or ... old Andronicus, plenty of blood and guts in that, about
as clean and tidy as a butcher's shambles. No?'

Palmer shook his head again. The bookseller sidled over,
putting his face closer to Palmer's.

'Perhaps sir wants something *saucier* – his Venus
discovered, ahem, nude, we've gone through several editions of
that, still very popular with the, mmm, discerning gentleman
reader. All the details, sir, very *exciting*.'

'I think I've got it,' Palmer pretended to remember. 'It's his
King Richard.'

The bookseller appeared overjoyed.

'"Now is the winter of our discontent, made *glorious* by
this sun of York." Everyone knows *that* one.'

Palmer contradicted him.

'The Second. King Richard the Second,' he repeated, 'The
Life and Death of.'

The bookseller looked around to check if anyone was
listening. He had the dangerous book, no question, but it was
buried in the back of his stall after all the uproar of Sunday last.

Palmer lowered his voice.

'Look,' he whispered, 'I must be the only one who wants to buy it, as things stand. But I must have the *full* text, you understand me?'

'The full text, yes sir, that is, as permitted by the licensing authorities.'

'So, not the...?'

'Not the...' the bookseller said, meaning the scene in which the king is deposed.

'It's all right, unofficial official business, if you know what I mean. Don't worry, you gave the right answer,' Palmer reassured him with a wink of the eye.

The bookseller looked at the shabby figure in front of him. He seemed unwilling to believe him.

'And you know the author, don't you?' Palmer went on.

'Well, no...'

'Come on! A man in your profession?'

'I mean, yes and no, that is, I used to, in the early days, when he was close to Mr Field.'

Publisher of the two books dedicated to Southampton, Palmer recalled and told the bookseller so.

'Yes, that's right sir, that's 'im. We have a regular arrangement, he has a highly respectable list – works of religious study, sir, translations of foreign classics, and only the best poetry.'

'That and the something *saucier*, I believe you said.'

The bookseller spread his hands in self-excuse.

'Sales patter, sir, you know how it is.'

'Where can I find this Field?'

The bookseller was only too keen to help if it meant getting rid of this awkward customer.

'Five minutes walk away,' he said, naming the street. 'Look for the sign of the Splayed Eagle.'

'About the book of the play,' Palmer began to say.

The bookseller looked fretful again.

'… I think I'll leave it this time.'

Blackfriars, then?

Not for the moment, Palmer decided, his satchel heavy and weighing on him. Instead he entered the cold, clammy interior of the great gothic Cathedral, pausing for a moment to watch the comings and goings inside. It was as busy as a marketplace, full of wheelings and dealings, some open, some furtive, none of the godly kind the building was intended for. It brought to his mind the story of the moneylenders in the temple.

He found a quiet alcove, in it a ledge on which to sit bathed by a ray of winter sun, dust-flecked all the way to the clerestory window through which it was streaming. Palmer pulled the sonnets out of his satchel, papers which could on the face of them be the brief of a lawyer preparing to meet a client, nothing out of place in this once sacred building.

He started to read.

'From fairest flowers we desire increase.'

He sighed. His eyes drifted up along the beam of light towards the unseen sun. Was that where heaven was? His father had believed in it, and in a burning, fiery furnace below. He too had believed in it once. And now?

For centuries the Palmers had gone with the grain and built up tidy estates. It was a carefully guarded inheritance which should have come to him – *would* have, if it hadn't been for the conscience of his father.

The holy fool! Palmer almost spat it out loud – the holy fool! Palmer senior who just *had* to go on professing the old faith, and in vehement terms too while the world was turning upside down replacing the old with the new. So he'd kept his soul – and lost the family estates. He'd died pure in conscience – and left his family destitute. Palmer was not impressed. Nor did he appreciate a God who did nothing for the son of such a foolish father. He felt instead for the reassurance of the purse against his chest. Hadn't he always sympathised with those moneylenders in the temple? Who needed a troublemaker bent on upsetting the order of things?

He allowed his eyes to drift down to the sheet in his hand.

'From fairest flowers we desire increase.'

He made himself read on. As he did, the poet's line of argument spoke quickly – that a young man should marry. There were the usual calls of duty, sonnet after sonnet of them, until a further reason intruded:

'Die single, and thine image dies with thee.'

Regular stuff, Palmer thought, about man's mortality and the only way to beat it, until the next claim came. It was so utterly astonishing that he read it twice.

'Make thee another self for love of me.'

For love of *him*? What was this? Life was a ladder of order and position, poverty serving prosperity, not the other way round. Poets did not command their patrons, did they? Certainly not country hicks from Warwickshire way!

How could it be explained? Was this perhaps a man of the world addressing a minor, the experienced speaking to the novice giving him the excuse to patronise youth? From the official report, Palmer remembered that Southampton had come of age seven years back.

Be that as it may, whatever the sonnets were saying, were they telling him anything of recent times, the times Cecil wanted to know about? Was the bond dead and buried or did it live on?

He took up a second book, of collected poems in which Cecil's official had marked out two sonnets. These were published just two years ago, Palmer remembered.

'When my love swears that she is made of truth,
I do believe her, though I know she lies.'

This was more like it – poets always had mistresses, cruel ones usually or what was there to moan on about? Even Palmer had once had one of the type, in his dim and distant past. He read on.

'My better angel is a man right fair,
My worser spirit a woman coloured ill.'

Not very kind to the lady.

'My female evil tempteth my better angel from my side.'

And what did this have to do with the price of hops, or the fate of a nobleman locked up in the Tower? The beam of illuminating light suddenly vanished, taking the words away from him. Palmer's bones were beginning to ache in the cold, winter air. He stood up to go. Questions were forming in his mind to ask Richard Field, Shakespeare's publisher in sonnet-time. The evidence he had just read proved nothing about the present.

An eating stall outside waylaid him. The attraction was a widow and her cooking.

'You're a stranger,' the woman said. 'Must be Easter last since we saw you.'

It puzzled Palmer how she always used 'we' when she habitually worked alone.

'Been busy, I'm sure, what with your *work*,' she went on.

Easter – he thought back. Yes, he'd been in funds, retained by an old Alderman jealous over his pretty young wife and not without reason. He'd managed to spin the case out for a whole month so there was money for Alice's famous pies, and an evening with her in a tavern, and a night with her in his bed.

'Don't think I've forgotten about it neither,' she said, leaving him in no doubt. 'What's a woman to think!'

'My *work*,' he pretended.

'Your work? Ha!'

He looked her up and down. It was not easy to place her age – not young, not yet of middle age. 'Buxom at board and bonner in bed' garbled its way into his memory, from the prayerbook his father had despised for talking of God in the common language.

'I called the child after you.'

Palmer frowned.

At sight of this, her face cracked into a great square-toothed grin.

'Nah, but it could've been for all you cared.'

Palmer hung his head in mock penitence.

'... and if I could've been sure you was the father!'

Palmer paid for a pie, biting into it with appreciation. A thought crossed his mind.

'You like the plays, don't you Alice?'

'I should say so! You invitin' me?'

Palmer ignored the remark.

'Does the name Shakespeare mean anything to you?'

Alice thought for a moment.

'Just a bit – not much of an actor, not like that lovely Dick Burbage; now there's a man I'd give my best pudding to an' with a double-filling!'

She gave Palmer a mischievous look.

'No, he's more of a *waddayacallit?*'

'Playwright?' Palmer suggested.

'That's it, playwriter, best one they've got – fills the playhouse, 'e does. I liked the one about the boy and girl and the friar, lovely it was, and sad, real tearful. So, is 'e in trouble? Must be if you're after 'im. Wouldn't surprise me...'

'Why's that?'

'They usually is, the actors – most irreg'lar – and what they gets away with saying on the stage!'

'Sedition, you mean?'

'Badmouthing, I calls it, or saying stuff out of season, that's the truth of it – what sounds well in spring goes down like a poisoned pie in winter. 'E liked my pies, mind.'

'Who?'

'Your Shake-it fella.'

'You mean you've come across him?'

'I've come across plenty,' Alice said with a glint in her eye. 'Shake-it used to be a regular with us when 'e lived this side of the water. 'E used to come round here,' she said, 'for books – reg'lar bookworm they said, them as knew 'im. And for my pies.'

'When he used to live this side of the river, you said...'

'They says 'e's gone over to the other side, when the playhouse moved there. Bankside's where you'll find 'im nowadays, over the river.'

'So what is he like?' Palmer asked.

'Now then. Hot 'n' cold, if you know what I mean, friendly – no, not in that way, more gentlemanlike, but not one you could get close to, if you knows what I mean, kept 'isself to 'isself. Very ... appreciative...'

Palmer laughed.

'... of my *pies*, you rogue. There was never none o' that. Pity in a way. Good-looking man, thin on top but that's never bothered me personally. Very clean, Mr Shake-it.'

'Shakespeare,' Palmer corrected her.

''Course I know *that*. It was my name for 'im, a joke between us, I do it with plenty of my customers, them as I like.'

'What's your name for me?' Palmer asked.

'Who said I liked *you*?'

The woman who came to the door of the printing works in Blackfriars when Palmer finally got there, full of Alice's pie, was not young. She told him in a foreign accent mixed with London riverside that her husband wasn't there.

He shot a practised, casual look past her to check. He saw nothing but the busyness of typesetters, machine-minders, hand pressers, finishers, binders and stackers; no-one who appeared to be the master, Richard Field.

'If it's business, you can speak to me,' she said.

'Or to me, my dear.'

The fresh voice which Palmer heard came from the street behind him. It was a well-to-do businessman's voice. When he turned round to see, Palmer took in a dapper man of about forty, soberly but expensively dressed with a touch of the dandy in the slashed sleeves and expensive silk linings; a man who liked to show how well he was doing.

'It's a private matter,' Palmer said.

Man and wife held their ground.

'Government business, in connection with Mr William Shakespeare,' Palmer persisted. 'I understand you know him.'

Field shot a sharp look of instruction to his wife. Grudgingly she stood aside.

'Follow me into the back room,' he murmured as he passed Palmer on the way in.

Once there, beyond the main workroom with its odours of wood, metal and ink mixed with the sweat of men, he closed the door behind him.

Palmer got straight to business.

'Tell me what you know about Mr Shakespeare. How long have you known him?'

Field coughed awkwardly.

'I must make clear that it's some years since Will and I collaborated professionally.'

Good, Palmer thought. Field was determined to distance himself from the word go – such a man would talk.

'When was that?'

Field appeared to think for a moment, the mark of someone, Palmer judged, who would make sure that the little things were correct in case he had to lie about the big ones.

'Oh, four, five years ago, back in '96. We did the third edition of his *Venus & Adonis* – and a good seller it was, too.'

'You come from the same town, you're of a similar age.'

'You're well-informed. I'm a couple of years older. Our families were neighbours, did business together. My father tanned hides, old man Shakespeare was in the luxury skins market – he made gloves. He was Chief Alderman, for a time.'

'The town's leading citizen!' Palmer pretended to be impressed before he speculated a question: 'religious affiliations?' There had been Catholic malcontents among the insurgents, after all.

'Very much in tune with the new way. He had nothing to do with the old faith, quite the reverse. He supervised the whitewashing of the superstitious old frescoes in our Chapel.'

It struck Palmer as too pat.

'I see, yet this paragon of the new order, he sees his son go off to become, what, an actor? About as respectable as vagabonds and thieves according to the statutes. How do you explain that?'

'John Shakespeare fell on hard times. That was, let me see, in the late '70s, about the time I was apprenticed up here in London – my wife, by the way, is the widow of my old master … a Huguenot.'

Palmer took the political reference at once. Huguenots were Protestants forced out of France by massacre and persecution. There was to be no suspect odour of the old faith about Richard Field, either that, or it had all been neatly tidied away.

'So, what went wrong?' Palmer asked.

'Old John was a man to make money when times were good but not when they weren't. Truth is,' Field confided with the air of one who did not make the same mistake,' he over-reached himself, loaned money to too many unable to pay him back. Then there was an important inheritance which was lost to the family.'

Field gave Palmer a significant look. Inheritances were important things. Palmer the disinherited understood it only too well.

'Yes, I'd almost forgotten,' Field said, 'it was his mother's dowry. Will never did – forget I mean. I would go so far as to say that he became obsessed by it. He tried twice in the London courts to get it back, in the '80s and then again in the '90s.'

'But you haven't told me what it was.'

'I'm sorry. It was good farming land, sixty, seventy acres if memory serves. It was his mother's as I said, from her father – they were Ardens, an important family in the county, yeoman stock though some, some are gentry.'

A second significant look. Palmer nodded without caring one way or the other. He was gentry himself. Little good it had done him.

Field quickly explained what had happened.

'John Shakespeare was running out of money so he mortgaged the land for ready cash to a relative thinking it would be safe. For some reason he didn't pay back the loan on the due day.'

'So the relatives took the title to the property?'

Palmer had heard it all before. He had acted for owners evicting defaulters with the same cynical ploy – lend the money, name a day, rely on the character of your debtor not to be able to pay you back. It is always the property you are after. It was the way of the world.

'Will never recovered the land, even when he had the money to pay for it.'

'You believe this was important?'

'Yes. It was symbolic, you see, property, the property that would begin to make him a gentleman. That was what his parents intended for him, right from the start.'

So, the Shakespeares had been set on becoming people of property...

'Still doesn't explain the acting,' Palmer said.

'Once his father failed, Will wasn't qualified for anything,' Field replied. 'He tried helping his father out but he was no tradesman. Then he was caught in the marriage trap – can't have been much more than eighteen, nineteen, and he had to earn money. He tried clerking and teaching but he could never stick at anything. Now I think about it, recovering the family land was his way of putting things right, putting *himself* right.'

'The court case here in London?' Palmer asked.

'It all started moving in '87. Heavens, what a year *that* was!'

Palmer agreed in silence – Mary, Queen of Scots executed for treason and Drake's attack on Cadiz to hobble the Spanish Armada building up on the Spanish coast towards invasion. It had translated the young Palmer from reluctant lawyer to volunteer soldier. Best days of his life, and those like him, the ones who survived!

'I was here in London finishing my apprenticeship when my master died,' Field said.

Yes, Palmer reckoned, Field looked the stay-at-home-and-make-money sort while others sweated and died in the trenches.

'So you did the usual, married the widow and took over the business,' Palmer said. 'You were able to help Shakespeare out with a roof over his head,' he guessed sensibly.

'No harm in that.'

'No harm at all.'

'He arrived with the Warwickshire levy – the Government was mobilising troops in the expectation of a Spanish invasion. He came to me when they disbanded. In return for board and lodge, he helped me in the works, read proofs, looked at new manuscripts, that sort of thing. The point is, Mr Palmer,' and here the printer gave his most significant look, 'Will was always bookish. It was *that* he was good at, always has been.'

'Really?'

'In my opinion, no-one loves books who doesn't come to them early.'

It sounded to Palmer like another practised statement. Field pressed on.

'We had books at school. For me, it was the look and feel of them. For Will, it was the words, especially poetry. There's a sonnet he wrote to the woman he married...'

Palmer was not interested in being waylaid by domestic details.

'Sonnets, yes, we know about them, we have a small store of them, found in the possession of Lord Southampton.'

The name of the arrested peer rattled ominously between them.

'Yes, well,' Field started to answer, 'it's obvious how that connection came about.'

In Stratford Susanna Shakespeare continued to watch her father like a young hawk. There had been all sorts of comings and goings to and from the house. One was at first unfamiliar so it had taken her a little time to recognise the man, a cousin whose father had owned the old family land her grandmother Mary talked about – the lost inheritance. She took the country cousin into the kitchen and plied him with ale.

'I be ready to talk 'bout selling the land back provided yowr da' an' me meets to discuss it outside Stratford – to avoid tittle tattle.'

Was this a time to be talking of land-buying, Susanna asked herself?

When she had got rid of the bumpkin she went in search of her father with the message. She found him looking round the garden, his eyes raised to the trees in his orchard, bare of leaves under a sky the colour of pewter. The mulberry was doing well, reaching out from the side of the house like the tentacle of a monster from the deep which, she had once heard him tell, sailors yarned about in the waterside taverns of London. The herb garden, her special charge, was as neat and tidy as she was herself.

The order of the cultivated plot pleased her with its evidence of steady growth from the cutting back, the budding, blossoming and fruiting of plants in their season, a cycle repeating, world without end. Until today she had assumed that this was the pattern of a life which would measure out her own days as well, one to be passed onto the children she had likewise assumed would one day be granted to her, and to their children coming after.

She watched her father kick aside a stone. Seeing her, he spoke.

'There is no better kingdom than a man's garden.'

Was that what kings said when forced to give up their kingdoms?

She gave him the message from the cousin. He showed no sign whether the news was good or bad. Instead they listened together to the few birds twittering in the otherwise silent space, tiny survivors safe from the majestic birds of prey – the eagle, hawk and falcon which he had often talked of seeing, what was it? 'Soar and swoop in search of prey in skies a world away,' away from Stratford, a world she now would never see? They too were the little birds, she reflected, she and the household here. A robin was bullying its way around the trees, coming close in the hope that the man might dig up easy pickings from the winter-hardened ground.

A thought made her father laugh out loud, a high, reckless sound which came flying out of nowhere as it did with all the men in the family. He did not share its meaning.

In Westminster Emilia Lanier was seeing to her boy. She gave orders to the maidservant about his care for while she was away for the night. It was some weeks until the quarter day when the girl should next be paid; she had a hold over her until then. She knelt down to look her boy in the eye.

'Henry, you will be a good boy while I'm gone?'

The boy nodded glumly.

'Remember our little secret?' she asked him, kissing him on the head.

His stepfather usually had a harsher opinion.

'You're giving him ideas, Emilia. The boy's a runt, an old man's spasm.'

He wasn't here now, thankfully. Even when he said this, the mother only turned away and smiled as if she knew different, knew better.

'Good!' she said now as the boy nodded back to her, promising to behave, 'then remember who you are.'

She ruffled his rich brown hair. Unseen by her, he put his tongue out at the maidservant who was pulling a face at him behind her mistress's back.

'Will first met the actors in Stratford,' Field was explaining to Palmer. 'They came through the town regularly. His father was the first local politician to license them.'

Palmer laughed, a rare sound.

'So, front row places for the Shakespeares at performances.'

'When he was old enough, he asked them for a job, trading on the old association.'

'Did they give him one?'

'Not immediately – actors will tell you there's a Will in every town, good-looking boys who've done a bit of acting, in school maybe or with the local town mummers. They fob them off with the usual – nothing available at the moment, need someone with experience, be delighted to see you in London if you ever get up to town.'

'So, was it in London then?'

'It was! Once he was settled with me, off he went to the plays. He made contact with some of his old acting mates, mainly the crowd round the Burbages – they'd played Stratford more than once. He claimed he could be useful to them since he was working for me – as if I'd touch their stuff! Anyway, they liked him, gave him a few menial jobs around the playhouse, the odd walk-on part...'

'From crowd extra to house poet to an Earl, it's a leap takes some explaining.'

Field gave Palmer a pained look, as if to say he was just getting to that.

'Will was word-struck from an early age – here with me he spent a lot of time looking at new work – no, not drama because we don't publish it, whatever he told the actors; other than that, you name it, we have it. He told me that it gave him an education he couldn't otherwise afford.'

'So what else was he reading?'

Field thought quickly.

'History chronicles, lives of the great classical figures, the art of poetry – we published a book on that as I recall – name of Puttenham mean anything to you?'

Palmer was not to be deflected.

'And he started *writing*, on his own account under your roof?'

'For all I know, he did. Now, throw in something else. The acting companies were in flux in the late '80s – threat of war, money was tight, companies were forming and re-forming, even going abroad for work...'

So they did, Palmer recalled, among the camp followers protected by their noble sponsors. He hadn't liked their work then any more than he did now.

'... there wasn't enough material for them to play, and those who produced it were freelancers who couldn't be trusted. You know, a regular trick of theirs was to sell a work to one company, wait till it went out on tour, then bold as brass, sell it to another.' Field insinuated another knowing look. 'They can be a shifty lot, authors,' he said, 'especially *that* generation. Kit Marlowe now – he came to a nasty end; who remembers him now?'

Palmer certainly didn't and had no intention of trying to.

'So Shakespeare, working for the actors, a writer on the side?'

'The actors wanted their own man. They were interested in someone who could brush up an old play, especially in times when money was short. If I remember correctly,' said Field who Palmer presumed to remember perfectly well, 'the theatre manager down at the Rose, over on Bankside, he had a rusty old Roman potboiler needed mending, nasty blood and guts stuff. I can do that, says William, and he did, and cheap too. Next time when the same man was having a problem with an unfinished play on the Wars of the Roses, he put Will in to rescue it. One play turned into three, and his name was made!'

So the tide had been in the man's favour, Palmer understood, who could only ever remember his own being on the way out.

'And Southampton?'

'Everyone who was anyone in London came to see those plays.'

'When was that?'

'In '90 or '91, I'd say.'

… when Southampton was fresh to London, resident at Grays Inn, a new star in the London sky. Ten years ago all the same, Palmer reminded himself. Best to push Field on.

'Of course Southampton came to the plays,' the printer said. 'All the bright young men did. He was impressed. He was in the process of gathering talent around him for the usual praise-singing of the noble patron. Will was gobbling up experience on every side.'

'And money too?'

'Money from writing, money from acting, private performances as well as public, and then, there were the gifts from his new friend, from Lord Southampton.'

Palmer's ears pricked up.

'You said *friend*. It's an unusual term to use to describe an actor in relation to the nobility.'

'Merely a turn of phrase.'

Palmer pursued it.

'The nature of the relationship between the two men, the *precise* nature?'

Field appeared to think carefully for a moment or two before speaking.

'I have seen at first hand, just once or twice, the sudden rise from nowhere of a new talent. There is nothing they can't do, no-one who doesn't want to meet them. It creates a certain commodity, maybe even a sort of equivalence, of talent with rank...'

Dangerous words, dangerous words, Master Field, Palmer said to himself. When Adam delved and Evie span, who was then the gentleman? Ideas such as these had fomented revolutions, crushed soon enough by the inexorable order of things, but not before heads were severed from shoulders and guts ripped out of unwilling bodies before a roaring mob.

'I mean, it wasn't long before Will's plays were put on at court,' Field said, 'while plenty of the big people booked private performances. It was a heady time and he was flying high – he came hurtling down to earth soon enough.'

'Why?'

'Plague. It closed the theatres for nigh on two years. It put all the actors out of work.'

Palmer only knew about it. Soldiering abroad had spared him the experience of it.

'The book trade wasn't spared either, I can tell you,' Field added hurriedly, 'except for our religious works. Religion always sells well in time of death and disaster,' he said, commercial satisfaction in his tone.

Palmer shut off the tap.

'Southampton is who I want to talk about. Why was the bond so special? Where do the sonnets fit in? Praise-singing duty, as you would call it?'

'Where do they fit in? Plenty of poets write songs of praise for their master. Will's sonnets were hardly a secret. Like most poets he circulated his work privately, although I believe one or two turned up in a published collection.'

'I have the book,' Palmer said, published two years ago, he called to mind. Was Field going to bring him closer? 'So how many sonnets were there?'

'How many have you got?'

Palmer tripled his score. Field's eyes narrowed, his laugh was acid.

'He wrote well over a hundred.'

Palmer covered his surprise.

'You said, in fact it was the very *first* thing you told me...'

'Yes?'

'... you said that you had not worked together, you and Shakespeare, for five years I think, after years of close collaboration.'

'That's right.'

'I find that difficult to believe. I mean, you're old friends, fellow townsmen, you put him up, help him on, publish two of his works – very handsomely too, I've got them with me – so what happened? Was he one of the ungrateful sort who forget their friends when the good times roll? Or did you argue?'

'Argue about what?'

'Money?'

Field drew back, offended.

'No, never! We pride ourselves in paying on the nail here.'

'But you don't deny that there was a rift.'

Field's temper began to fray.

'Look, we *do* publish poetry, we *don't* publish plays. After *Venus*, and *Lucrece*, Will didn't write any more poetry.'

'Except for the sonnets.'

'They were written well before, most of them.'

Over a hundred of them, private sonnets, prime, fashionable material from the pen of the biggest name around. What an opportunity, Palmer reckoned! Why wouldn't Field publish?

'There *was* a quarrel, I admit.'

Field appeared to clam up. Wait for it to come out, Palmer told himself. He was right – Field could not stay silent.

'Will's acting company took a property near us here in Blackfriars, part of a plan to open a private theatre to appeal to a higher class of audience. I ... I signed the petition against it.'

Did he now? Palmer believed him, he looked the type, the type who wouldn't hesitate to protect his own interests now he was a proper little city burgher on the way up. He was probably in the market for one of those dodgy coats of arms! But five years of nothing between poet and publisher while times moved on and both prospered? From the little Palmer knew of him, Field didn't sound like a quarreller, more like one who kept his doors – and his hands – open.

'Mr Field, I want those sonnets.'

Field spread his palms in helplessness. Palmer would not be put off.

'I want the sonnets, I believe you have them.'

'Ridiculous.'

'No,' Palmer said, 'several other possibilities, but not that one. Now if I'm right, a formal search by the Chief Minister's people ought to find them – a very thorough and a very *public* search.'

'Why – if I had them at all – why should I?' Field said at last.

'Your loyalty to your old friend is admirable,' Palmer flattered him, 'but holding onto them won't help him. I have orders to find him wherever he is, anywhere in the kingdom. He'll have a full set somewhere himself so it's only a matter of time and look at it this way – it won't sit well with the authorities if you could have helped us earlier.'

Field looked away for a few seconds.

'Manuscripts are very vulnerable,' he said at last. 'Will asked me to look after them, when he went away on tour – they are fair copies. If you give me a few moments I will look them out.'

As he went to where he knew they were, Field looked a worried man. He should have done the sensible thing, Palmer said to himself, his eyes following him.

He should have destroyed them long ago.

~ 5 ~

PALMER PAUSED for a moment outside the printing works he had just left. He took a deep breath of air. Putrefaction reached his nostrils instead. He laughed quietly at the reminder. The laughter turned to frowning at the thought of having to read the wad of newly discovered sonnets jammed into his satchel.

A woman's voice interrupted him.

'You want some, luvvie?'

Palmer looked up. She was young, not much more than a girl. White paste covered a smallpox-ravaged face out of which small black eyes, glazed by liquor, stared unsteadily at him.

Walk on, he told himself.

He felt her hand on his wrist. He knew all the lines – amorous, begging, father and mother dead or baby at home.

Walk on.

'Oy, you!'

The aggressive male voice stopped him in his tracks. Its owner was big, shaven-headed, trouble.

Walk on, walk on.

'You, you 'eard the little lady.'

Palmer knew the form – purchase the goods or pay her off. If not, risk a good hiding. He heard the bolt shut loudly on the entrance to the printing works behind him. Field wanted no trouble. Didn't mind if he, Palmer, got a face full. How neighbourly!

'How much?' he asked.

It was worth sixpence or a shilling not to put the papers he had collected at risk. The man in front of him – her pimp, her brother, both? – grinned.

'We'll settle for *whatever* you've got to offer.'

Suddenly the girl was gone, the street was deserted. Palmer sensed his skin prickle. The man in front of him was fingering a cosh. An old anger stoked up inside. Surrender the fee he'd got from the Chief Minister? Give up his security? Damned if he would...

Palmer dropped his satchel and picked up a stone. He hurled it at the goliath striking him firmly on the chest. A roar of rage announced a clumsy charge forward. Palmer turned cold and calm. At the last second he dodged the onrush and threw all his weight behind a punch. He felt his knuckles sink in to the man's throat, felt the resistance and then something give way against it.

The man staggered, stopped, began to choke. He collapsed to the ground. Palmer waited until the strangled sounds subsided then he turned the body over with his foot. A mottled, purple face, eyes bulging wide and lifeless, stared up at him. The grotesque comedy of it brought him back into the present.

He looked around him – there were no witnesses that he could see. He walked decisively on, looking back from time to time, the mound of flesh growing smaller and smaller. The man lay still where he had fallen. The girl was nowhere to be seen. As the river came into view, Palmer began to lay suspicion aside – it was nothing more than a nasty, chance encounter. There was no-one on his case, was there?

The waterman who picked Palmer up was one of the doggedly talkative sort.

'Play'ouses closed,' he announced, once they were well out into the stream and his sixpenny fare over to Bankside was guaranteed. 'Bad for business o' course. Reckon as I takes 'undreds over there. Tha'sands. And back. Don't see what they see in it meself. Load o' nonsense if you ask me.'

Palmer thrust his hands under his armpits to protect them from the cold feeding up from the black, shining water. He flexed his right hand – nothing broken.

He asked the waterman a question.

'How was business Saturday afternoon?'

It was the day of the Richard play at the Globe to which he was headed.

'A bit thin, if you ask me.'

'What sort of people?'

'Usual types, apprentices who ought to be apprenticin', wives from the City who ought to be wivin', a few young bucks out on the looksee.'

'Any of the better class sorts?'

'Yeah, yeah, maybe more o' them than usual.'

'Recognise any of them?'

'Nah, they all look the same to me. Mouthy types, you know, all swagger an' no sense. Been a lot o' them abaht lately.'

He looked at his passenger.

'You the law?'

The look he got from Palmer shut his mouth for the rest of the crossing.

Palmer found the actors' entrance to the theatre easily enough. It was the only one open. The Globe was otherwise deserted, closed until further notice by the authorities after the events of the weekend. Bands of soldiers were enforcing the order.

From the closed-up Bear Garden next door, angry barking betrayed dogs penned up in their kennels which were trained to bait bears. Palmer felt sorrier for them than for the actors. They had no say in their employment.

The Globe doorkeeper was taciturn. No, Mr Shakespeare was not there. No, nobody else was there either.

'Who's in charge, then?'

The doorkeeper gave him a closer look and saw the clenching fist.

'Who's askin'?'

Palmer's fist relaxed to slip him a small coin.

'It's Gus Phillips you want,' the man said.

'I expect he drinks round here.'

Palmer was given the names of two inns, the George and the White Hart. Something in the answer told him that it was right but just not right today. He set off, walking parallel with the river on his left, looking for a drinking hole within a stone's throw of the theatre, not the fanciest but the most convenient. He found it in minutes, low and unmarked, an ordinary alehouse. He went in.

A momentary arrest in the general conversation told him that those inside weren't strangers to each other and knew that he was. In a loud voice, he told the landlord who he wanted. Another voice spoke up from a dark recess at the back.

'*Augustine* Phillips,' the voice insisted. 'Who wants him?'

Palmer took his pot of beer to the table where the voice had come from. He found a dark, sharp-featured type in the company of a second burlier man. The fox and the bear, Palmer couldn't help thinking.

He introduced himself but not his business. Phillips was cool. The other man went by the name of John Hemmings. He looked the easier-going of the two on the large-boned, ruddy face of it; a deceptive appearance, Palmer suspected.

'I haven't come to commission another special performance,' he said quietly. The nervous strain on Phillips's face increased; Hemmings's remained unflustered, an act of great control.

Phillips spoke first.

'We have no intention of, of...'

'... being an accessory to another act of treason?' Palmer suggested. 'My masters will be happy to hear it. Once was quite enough, only they want me to find out *why* it happened.'

Hemmings interrupted. He spoke in a grave bass voice.

'And your masters are? We, you see, are the Lord Chamberlain's Men.'

Palmer rocked back then sat briskly forward, arms on the table, threat evident.

'Well, the Chief Minister is of the opinion that one of your company was Lord Southampton's man, the same Southampton who is presently locked up in the Tower for leading an armed insurrection against Crown and State; whose *friends* were apparently generous enough to pay your company, your *Lord Chamberlain's* Men, to perform an old play dealing with revolution and the murder of a king.'

Hemmings's glance towards Phillips looked full of warning.

'We have given our version of events already,' Phillips said, 'and it's the truth.'

'Tell it to *me* this time.'

'Why should we?'

'Because I have in my possession a batch of sonnets, sonnets taken from Southampton's lodgings by official search. I've spent the day collecting others. Now they show a bond of some *closeness* between his lordship and his man in your company, and what do you know – the man in question, he's up and left town!'

The two men exchanged uncomfortable looks. Hemmings let Phillips reply.

Phillips set out on his story, already well practised Palmer judged, how the actors had been approached the week before by some of the Earl of Essex's men.

'They wanted us to put on the old Richard play, for one performance only.'

Hemmings backed his colleague up.

'We didn't find it out of the ordinary. The well-to-do often pay for special performances. In this case we made sure that they paid extra because we weren't at all sure that there would be much of an audience for such an old piece; which goes to show,' he added, as if the thought had just occurred to him, 'that our behaviour was in no way political.'

'So you are saying that what was in the play never crossed your mind. Your concern was all about the money.'

'Exactly,' Hemmings agreed.

'How much did you get for it?'

Phillips answered.

'Forty shillings in addition to the take on the door.'

'Hmmm, ten silver pieces more than Judas.'

Phillips surged forward in sudden anger. Palmer shoved him back. His right hand itched. He saw that Hemmings saw it. Hemmings put an arm around his colleague's shoulder. The smile on the big man's face was narrow, quizzical.

Palmer spoke to him.

'Shakespeare now, what part did he play in all this?'

'Oh, he wasn't here.'

'Wasn't here when? For the performance?'

'No.'

'When the sponsors came to arrange the play?'

'Not at the Globe, no, Gus and I handle the business side of things.'

'Then, you will know where he is now.'

'Stratford!' Phillips said, anger still bristling in his voice. 'In Warwickshire! It's where he comes from!' Then he calmed a little. 'He had word that his father is gravely ill.'

'It's true,' Hemmings weighed in. 'The old man's past seventy. I met him once, back in the '80s, when I was on tour in Stratford...' and he was away, boasting how it was he who had backed the young Shakespeare, brought him on 'and I don't care who knows it!'

'Tell me more about Shakespeare and ... Southampton,' Palmer asked. 'I know how they met and how the sonnets started. What I want to know is – what's the latest story between them?'

'What if there is no story?' Phillips blazed back.

There is always a story, Palmer's eyes told him.

Hemmings appeared to take the hint.

'We had Will working in a good vein of history plays, powerful stuff, popular with our bread and butter market, popular with the well-to-do, so long as we didn't upset them by insulting their ancestors! Then along comes Southampton. At first we thought he was harmless, money for old rope, but that wasn't what the noble *prick* had in mind, leastwise not for his tame poet.'

'What do you mean?'

'He wanted Will to try his hand at comedies set in colourful locations – Sicily, Padua, Athens, Verona. Just names to the likes of us.'

'To be fair to him,' Phillips interrupted, his temper cooling, 'they turned out every bit as good and popular too. Southampton reckoned we should be grateful.'

His voice took on a renewed note of complaint.

'... he went round telling his fine friends that he'd made Will the writer he was!'

'And us the top company,' Hemmings reminded him.

'And this was after '94?' Palmer cut in.

'No, no, before. Southampton was at Will well before, right from the start.'

'To do what?'

'To stop prostituting himself before the hoi polloi, was how he put it. It was hardly likely to endear him to us.'

'In fact,' Hemmings said, taking over, ''94 was a time of respite for us all round, and from Southampton.'

'Why was that?'

'Simple, he came of age. He went off on a military career so we hoped we'd seen the last of him. With a bit of luck, the lad would go and get himself killed!'

Palmer did not laugh at the joke.

'You *hoped?* It wasn't how it turned out, was it?'

'No. It wasn't the last we saw of him – not that I'd place too much weight on it,' the actor put in hastily.

'And why not?'

'Well, Southampton was busy trying to get his military career started, and as for Will, he was busy in his own work, we all were. It was an astonishing time.'

Phillips took over.

'To cap it all, the lease on our theatre in Shoreditch expired. We didn't have much time for Southampton then, or him for us, we were all too occupied looking after ourselves.'

'What happened next?' Palmer asked Hemmings.

'Oh, we formed a new syndicate, and when the landlord started playing clever clogs over the lease, we dismantled our theatre lock, stock and barrel – remember Gus, all that snow falling and the frozen river? We eventually shipped the whole lot over the Thames here to Bankside. We created our very own Globe as you now doubt know it...'

The look on Palmer's face disabused him but Hemmings wasn't to be stopped.

'... *totus mundus agit histrionem* – that's our motto written up on the wall. It's Latin, for *all the world's a stage.*'

A very loose translation, Palmer reckoned. He had another, more important question.

'When was that?'

'A couple of years ago.'

'It kept Will busier than ever because the first season was make or break for us,' said Phillips.

'We brought over Harry Five; Julius Caesar, now that was written to open the Globe itself and then there was a pastoral set in the forest...'

'And where was Southampton all this while?'

'Most recently,' Hemmings said, 'away on the Irish campaign.'

'But I take it that you did see him from time to time?'

'In between campaigns, yes, I suppose we did.'

'He was here quite a lot, last year,' Phillips reminded Hemmings, 'when he wasn't welcome at court.'

'A bit like the old days, was it?'

Hemmings attempted to laugh the inference off.

Palmer had what he wanted, grounds for a continuous association. He changed the subject.

'And what is your man's latest play?'

Phillips shifted uneasily on his stool.

'A play called *Hamlet.*'

'Comedy is it?'

Palmer made his way back across the Thames by boat in the late afternoon, mulling over what he had learned. So there had been recent contact between Shakespeare and Southampton. Would Cecil welcome what he had unearthed? Should he tell the client the truth, or what he wanted to hear?

He wasn't ready to go home yet. He directed the waterman, thankfully a silent one, to the north bank and Temple stairs just below London's legal district. The light was fading, the cold intensified. He heard the church bells din out their competing chimes. It came as no surprise to him that the capital was never quiet.

He took a brisk walk up Middle Temple, heading towards Chancery Lane.

When he got there, he found his man, as the porter told him he would, walking in the gardens of Lincoln's Inn. William Lambarde was wrapped in a heavy cloak and in contemplation of some fine legal point, no doubt.

Palmer approached his old tutor cautiously across an interval of twenty years. He was conscious of his shabby appearance, symbol of a failure to prosper, anathema to the legal spirit which prized success over everything including, some said, justice.

The old man saw him coming.

'Palmer, Richard Palmer, isn't it?' he said with the uncanny memory of the teacher.

Palmer felt the man's eyes on his threadbare clothes. Was he steeling himself for a call on his charity? The thought embarrassed him. Quickly he took the old man into his confidence. Lambarde appeared to relax. Palmer knew he would not be the last lawyer or the first to end up in the world of secret intelligence. It would explain the clothes, he told himself, fit for the underworld in which he was moving.

'How may I help you?' Lambarde asked.

Palmer dealt rapidly with the Richard play, pausing on the name of its author.

'I believe you knew this Shakespeare, over a family inheritance case,' he said.

Lambarde looked away, sniffing the air.

'A bad business, a bad business. They will put their best lawyers onto it, Coke of course, he's the Attorney-General, and clever little Francis Bacon, he's begging for the job.'

'I beg your pardon?' Palmer was taken aback.

'The trial, Essex, Southampton and all the rest. Of course it will be proved, the evidence is clear. What will the charges be? Conspiracy at the least, high treason in all probability, threatening the life of the Queen and her ministers in person, attempting to overthrow the State.'

Palmer sensed himself back in the tutorial room and its dry debate. Lambarde's voice trotted on.

'And the performing of the play? It could only be unlawful if the text was in some way unauthorised, say unlicensed, or in some other way proscribed, wouldn't you say? I understand that the original script was properly licensed, even if its later publication suffered cuts – the royal deposition scene I mean, in which Richard surrenders his crown...'

Ah, but that was then and this is now, Palmer wanted to say, the politics of it had changed as might the law. He held his tongue.

'... of course the performance could be deemed unlawful if it formed part of a conspiracy, an intention to commit a criminal act.'

All modern drama is a criminal act, Palmer told himself.

'... a criminal act, yes, such as to incite rebellion, wouldn't you say, Richard?'

The use of his first name, the teacher's privilege, took Palmer by surprise. So did what Lambarde said next.

'... excellent man, Shakespeare, terrible case, most unjust, most unjust. I suggested he try again in Chancery since he failed in the first action at Queen's Bench.'

Where was Lambarde now? Back to the old family inheritance case. Keep up, Palmer told himself.

'There they are bound by precedent, you see, bound to interpret the strict letter of the law. The land was mortgaged, there was an explicit bond, the loan was not repaid in the way the bond required so it was not correctly discharged. Their hands were tied, plain and simple.'

'And yours were not?'

'In Chancery we are more *equitable*, let us say, we bring natural justice to bear. And we take a dim view of sharp practice where settlement is denied on a narrow point.'

'And it was in this case?'

'Order and prosperity in society are based on property, its secure enjoyment and safe transmission. There was dispute between the parties about when the money needed to be ready.'

The lawyer's eyes twinkled with mischief.

'Of course, I could take no part in the proceedings. You see, I *knew* the plaintiff, Shakespeare.'

Did he now! At last!

'What sort of man is he?' Palmer asked.

'Most interested in the law.'

It was Lambarde's first rule of character, Palmer recalled, the prism through which he saw the world.

'Knowledgeable as well, some country legal training in him I shouldn't wonder. I gave him a copy of one of my books, he was very pleased to receive it. Ooh yes, I knew Shakespeare, met him in the inns of court – Gray's Inn, now I come to think of it. They are *great* presenters of plays, you know. Are you interested in the drama, Richard?'

Palmer suppressed a sharp reply. Instead he asked another question.

'Wasn't he mixed up with the Earl of Southampton there?'

'Well I know nothing about *that*.'

Lambarde's response was dismissive – because the Earl was never serious about the law?

'Shakespeare's case – you know he wrote a play about it?' he said instead.

It was a play about a Jew, he told Palmer, who loaned money to a merchant so that the merchant could help a younger friend, 'a dear friend,' Lambarde said, who was chasing an heiress.

Palmer's ears perked up at the nature of the men's relationship.

'Unwise, unwise,' the lawyer said, probably about the lending of the money.

The collateral was the merchant's ventures overseas. The Jew joked that if his ships did not come in he would accept, as compensation, a pound of his flesh.

A playful sign of his trust or something more sinister? Palmer was not sure he cared.

The ships were reported lost, the debtor could not repay.

'Not on the *due date*,' Lambarde emphasised, 'even though his friend, having secured his heiress offers to pay the debt many times over. No, the Jew insists on his *strict bond*.'

'Why would he do so? ' Palmer asked, wondering where this was all leading.

'The dramatist would have us think that it has to do with the abduction of the Jew's daughter and all his gold by friends of the merchant, but I say that this is irrelevant to the legal point we must consider. Can the Jew rely on his bond? Must he have his pound of flesh?'

Palmer continued to look mystified.

'So, Richard, how would you plead the merchant's case?'

Palmer was tempted to say that in his world other, darker methods would be employed before the matter reached court. He groped towards a guiding principle.

'Natural justice cannot allow physical injury to be inflicted over a civil obligation. Blood debt no longer exists in law.'

'Perhaps so, perhaps so,' the lawyer conceded. 'The dramatist makes a fine scene of just such a line of approach, based on mercy, but it does not succeed, no, it does not.'

'So how is it resolved?'

'Most ingeniously, most ingeniously.'

Lambarde patiently explained.

'The Jew is permitted his pound of flesh. The flesh may be *cut* provided – and this is very good,' the old man chuckled, 'provided no *blood* is drawn. Why? Because the bond does not *stipulate* blood, only flesh. It is the very strictest interpretation of the bond which wins the day! The biter is bit! Mr Shakespeare would have made a most ingenious advocate!'

'And when was this written?'

'Four years ago?' Lambarde supposed.

The date interested the investigator. And the sacrificial theme – older man for younger, in pursuit of marriage, marriage which the sonnets laboured so hard to commend – echoed another bond, the one between Shakespeare and Southampton.

Together with what the actors had told him about Southampton's attendance at the plays right up to recent times, it was another puncture in Cecil's hope, for evidence of separation in the distant past. And what a witness, a celebrated judge and master of law!

'So you go to the plays?' Palmer asked in an attempt to bring the conversation onto lighter ground.

'Ooh yes, anything by Shakespeare for preference.'

'The Richard play?'

'Of course, at a private performance. A lot of important people were there, the Chief Minister for example,' Lambarde said, raising what looked like an ironic eyebrow.

Not something Cecil had thought to tell him, Palmer reflected.

'What did you make of it?'

'You have seen, or read it?'

It was the question Palmer had most feared in his student days.

'Bad monarch deposed by a better man?' he suggested.

Lambarde thought about it for a moment.

'And yet, Richard gains our sympathy in the end ... which is what surprised me about the performance on Saturday at the Globe.'

Palmer stopped dead in his tracks. The old fox!

'You were there?'

'Why not? It was too good an opportunity to miss. Not that I would dare say as much to our Queen. She is mightily offended, let me tell you – by that scene where Richard must give up his crown to the usurper Bolingbroke. She told me so herself. I am her archivist, you know, at the Tower. One of my several responsibilities.'

'Is she right to be? Offended?'

'It was all a bit rusty, the voice of the prompter was heard abroad more than one might have wished. Yet Burbage was excellent as Richard. As to the meaning of the play and the Queen's response to it, I have one question.'

'Which is?'

'Has she ever seen it? I do not believe she has. Taken all in all, a rabble-rouser it is *not* in my humble opinion. We are made by the author to suspect that the usurpation will bring great pain, which is why I was surprised.'

'By what?'

'... by the insurgents' choice of it.'

~ 6 ~

WHAT REMAINED of the day's light gave little help to walkers on Fleet Street, the gate to the walled City ahead of them veiled in gloom. Through upstairs windows candles were flickering. Here and there at street level a flaming brand was leading a party home.

Palmer had little desire to go back to Clerkenwell. Another visit to the Bell Inn instead? It was on a wider sweep home even if it meant passing through the city gate around curfew, the same gate the Essex crew had galloped through, was it only yesterday?

In his undecided state, his eye was caught by a single figure, slight, hooded, cloak bulked out by a woman's dress underneath, gliding cautiously through the dusk. After the dry-as-dust conversation with Lambarde, he was feeling an old itch.

No respectable woman would be out unaccompanied at this time of night. His mind quickly discarded the memory of the street girl outside Field's printing works. He decided to try his luck with this one backed by the power of his refilled purse. As he moved he saw the woman check, as if she was thinking of crossing over to the other side despite the foulness of the gutter.

He stood in her way.

'Let me pass,' she demanded, in unexpected court tones.

There was nothing of the street about them. They transfixed Palmer, like a voice he thought he had forgotten. He pulled back the woman's hood.

'Emilia?

She looked up at him, her voice trying to conceal her fear.

'Mrs Lanier, wife to *Captain* Lanier. Do I know you?'

He recognised the upturned face, the first wave of jet-black hair just visible under her cap. Her features had a leaned, chiselled look, pared down since youth. Still, there was no mistaking her.

'You used to,' he said, 'in Kent – Richard Palmer.'

'I remember you,' she said at last.

It was not easy to entertain a woman respectably in public. Even Palmer knew that taverns or eating houses were not places for women of decent reputation. A church, however, would serve the purpose. He took Emilia firmly by the arm as he led her through a heavy, oaken door.

The light in the church was obscure, only a few candles burning and stinking with their fatty smell of liquidising tallow. Niches empty of statues and walls whitewashed to conceal the coloured cartoons of martyred saints somehow deconsecrated the space, even in the mind of an unbeliever like Palmer. An old, incomprehensible anger was stoking up inside him. Questions were piling up inside his head. What was Emilia's story since she returned to London? One look at her told him that Captain Lanier, whoever he was, was only the half of it. What was she doing out on her own at this time of night?

The answer she gave, about a visit to her doctor, did not convince him. When she gave him his name – Forman – a little light gathered in his mind. The man was a low-life, an astrologer, a dubious meddler with other men's women – he had once followed the Alderman's wife there, asked questions, got dubious answers. Was Emilia on the street for the old reason? He had seen better as well as worse forced to that extreme.

Early days came back to him – his when the Palmers enjoyed their Kentish house and lands, hers in the household of a noblewoman in that county. It had been a good situation for the daughter of a court musician who had died leaving his family unprovided. Italian, wasn't he? The girl turned out refined, he had discovered, visiting as a neighbour. He replayed their walks in pleasant gardens, taciturn on his part, talking much but saying little on hers. He saw – as if it was yesterday – her fingers play filigree music on a dainty keyboard. It never fell silent long enough – she never let it, he realised across the years – to let him say to her what he had rehearsed; awkward masculine words of love.

The time came when word arrived that her mother had died and she was an orphan.

'When I returned to London, I came to the notice of one of the most important families in the country,' he heard her say now in the cold, spiritless air of the church.

A powerful man, he heard himself guessing.

'I was taken into their service.'

Into his bed.

'They found me a good husband, a handsome military officer.'

When her protector died, when she had outlived her purpose?

'We have a son of seven, a good-looking boy, but we lost a daughter. Isn't it all such a world away, those days in Kent?'

Yes it was, Palmer admitted to himself but he saw the reality in front of him. She was a woman who had seen better days, out after dark without protection. Was she really going to Forman to gain some hope about her future? Or for another kind of payment?

She carried on talking. She did not ask him his story. Then she made a move to leave.

Palmer gripped her arm with his hand, the one which had killed in the morning, holding her back.

Her courage appeared to reassert itself.

'Let me go, Dick.'

The words froze him in the act. They were the same she had used all those years ago when she told him she would go back to London.

He loosened his grip.

'So you turned me down for the bed of an old man, Milly.'

Her mouth opened as if to deny it before her mind changed.

'A rich and powerful man, Lord Hunsdon, the Lord Chamberlain. I had everything I wanted.'

Dead now, all the same, replaced by his son in name, title and court position. So it went...

She began to recite what it had brought her. Brutally he interrupted her, told her his current case, spat out the name – Southampton – a name she didn't seem to want to hear by the way she put her finger to his lips as if to force the word back.

'So his life is in your hands,' she said, keeping her finger in place.

The darkness in Palmer's tenement chamber forgave the passing of their years. Like a gauze, it shaded the reality, screening out imperfections. For Palmer there were moments when, seeing the outline of her face below his, he saw her as she once was.

They fell apart, unsatisfied.

He half-closed his eyes, saw that she was awake, watching, waiting to do what? He didn't know. He felt her move, putting distance between their sweating bodies. When the chamber window began to appear more distinct in the darkness, he saw her silently slip out of bed to dress. A pale shaft of light disclosed his satchel and her, quietly and expertly exploring inside it. Did she think he would be foolish enough to leave money in it?

She pulled out a sheet, moving it into adequate light. He heard her catch her breath. She appeared to toy with the idea of taking the satchel. Then she looked over towards him – he didn't move. Once again she looked at the sheet in her hand, as if she was trying to calculate its value. Was it coincidence they had met? Was someone using her, placing her deliberately in his way? He saw her take more sheets, more sonnets, not so many he might notice but enough – for what?

He stilled the desire to stop her. He needed to know who she was working for. Why not beat it out of her? Why so precious about her? His eyes followed her creeping to the door of the chamber, turning the key in the lock before disappearing without a backward glance. He threw on his clothes with practised speed. He reached the street in time to see her turning the far corner.

It was close to an hour before Emilia arrived at her house beside the ditch.

Palmer watched her go into the house from across the way. The husband couldn't be around, he reckoned or she wouldn't have spent the night away. There might be a servant. Sure enough, a girl came out pulling a small boy in tow, on his way to school. Palmer looked the boy over. He was unremarkable, except for unruly hair fighting its way out from under his cap.

Once the pair were out of sight, Palmer made his way round to the back of the house. He let himself in without a noise. The only sound he heard inside was a woman's. He followed it to the kitchen. Emilia had her back to him, singing softly, poking the embers of the fire. Hell! Was she burning the sonnets? He stepped up sharply behind her to stop her, stronger hand on weaker wrist.

She gave a startled gasp.

'The servant girl, when does she come back?' Palmer demanded.

'Soon.'

It was a lie, he was sure.

'And your husband?'

'Any time now.'

Palmer did not believe her. He pushed Emilia down roughly, pulling up a second stool so that he could confront her face to face.

'Who sent you after me?'

Emilia appeared bewildered.

He took a closer look at her in the clearer morning light – at the signs of age, the hair too jet for the dark brown it had been, the forehead lined, creases around the eyes and a downward droop to the mouth.

'Who sent you after me?' he repeated.

She blew out her cheeks, exhaling a short, frustrated breath.

He raised a hand as if to strike her. All he got was a look of contempt. Lanier beat her, he bet.

'Southampton?' he asked, 'or his people?'

She started up. He forced her back down. Southampton, he asked himself? How was it she was tied in with him?

She was old Hunsdon's piece, that much he knew. And Hunsdon? Lord Chamberlain, patron of the actors. One of those actors was Shakespeare...

Flares went off in his head, lines of sonnet verse hammered inside his brain.

'*My better angel is a man right fair*

My worser spirit a woman coloured ill.'

The words came involuntarily.

'You were Southampton's...'

'Whore?' she shot back.

He added it all up – old Lord Hunsdon, creeping his way towards death which left her unprovided; Southampton smiling promises in return. Not a wise choice.

And Shakespeare, how did Shakespeare come into it? A go-between? Paid how?

Palmer began to guess. 'As you say,' he said, 'and Shakespeare's too? It's what those sonnets tell us, isn't it?'

He saw Emilia shudder at the reminder. No, Milly would be damned if she'd own up to a Shakespeare. She'd done her time with an old man, it was time for her to taste youth. And then what? The child most like, a baby on the way. Hunsdon couldn't get rid of her quickly enough – passing her on, at a cost, to Lanier. The boy was seven, the dates added up.

'We both know these sonnets involve you with one traitor, and maybe with another. Milly, I told you who my client is, the Chief Minister.'

She gave Palmer no answer.

'What do you call the boy?' he asked her.

'Henry,' she said then, seeing his look of surprise, 'no, he's not Southampton's. He was named after Henry, Lord Hunsdon. I should know whose he is.'

Palmer did not believe her. Years of being kept by the old Lord Chamberlain, a man well into his sixties, and suddenly she falls pregnant?

'So Hunsdon had you married off to a nobody to give the bastard a name. Back to where you came from, Milly.'

Emilia straightened her back.

'My husband is an officer who fought bravely against the Spaniards.'

'Led by men – Essex and the rest – who count for nothing now.'
He looked around at the pokey surroundings.

'I can see how life is with you.'

'And your rathole has more to recommend it?' she flared back.

'No,' he admitted. 'So tell me, when did all this business between you, Shakespeare and Southampton happen?'

She kept her memories to herself.

Palmer tried a different approach.

'Face facts – the winner out of all of this is William Shakespeare. He got it all – fame, a fortune from his trade, compared to ... what?'

He looked around the room. A thought came into his mind.

'Did he write you anything?'

Emilia Lanier opened and then shut her mouth. She appeared to be calculating her choices.

'There are about a dozen of them – sonnets, if that's what you mean...'

'In addition to the ones you took from me this morning.'

'They're all in my chest upstairs. If we can agree a price, I'll be pleased to have them out of the house.'

He offered her a figure beyond what she expected, a tithe of what she had once been worth.

'Promise me one thing, for my boy's sake,' she asked after she handed the papers over. 'He needs his stepfather. Please tell the Chief Minister how helpful we Laniers have been.'

~ 7 ~

IT WAS NEARLY MIDDAY before Cecil was free to see his agent.

Palmer made his report – there was a strong and personal relationship between poet and patron, longer and deeper than had been thought and lasting. They had shared a mistress, evidenced by the sonnets he had uncovered.

Cecil's eyebrows rose when he was told the woman's name and the request she made for amnesty for her husband.

'Lanier is Essex's man, but he's a minnow. I'll have his name taken off our lists.'

'The actors by the way, they had no idea what the insurgents were using them for.'

Cecil made a precautionary note to summon them to repeat this in front of the Privy Council.

The information about an illness to Shakespeare's father in Stratford came next.

'How fortunate,' the politician said, 'so we know where he is.'

'What do you want me to do now?' Palmer asked.

'Confront Shakespeare directly.'

Palmer was surprised. If Cecil wanted Southampton exonerated, wasn't he going an odd way about it?

'So, Stratford then?'

'As I told you, we shall put Essex and Southampton on trial Thursday week which leaves us nine days. Stratford is normally, let me see, three days journey out, the same back, unless you are a practised horseman?'

The look Palmer gave was intended to disabuse him.

'Then you must leave today. I will issue you with the necessary warrant in case he won't come willingly. Make sure you bring him back,' the Chief Minister ordered.

A summons from the Queen was brought in by Cecil's chief official. It was plainly not what Cecil was expecting. Palmer was quickly ushered out of the man's presence and sent on his way.

Cecil went immediately to the Queen's privy chamber where she conducted confidential business. Her favourite lady-in-waiting, one of her own generation, gave the politician a warning look. It said that her mistress the Queen had something on her mind.

'Well, little man...'

Such was the Queen's style of address to him! It was better than 'pygmy' which she had once had the taste for calling him despite his standing as her senior minister. The world knew that Cecil must make his way by other than physical prowess. It was why he had followed the course set by his father – of politics before the sword. What Cecil lacked in physical force he made up for in his knowledge of people and how to play them.

His face appeared to smile gracefully at the Queen's diminutive greeting.

'How are we getting on?' she asked him, about the insurrection.

He repeated what she already knew – the date of the first trial which he had just shared with Palmer, and the other trials they had in hand. But another question, so far unspoken, hovered between them.

'This brings me to my point,' he said.

A barely visible royal eyebrow arched in expectation. The game between them was an old one.

'Your Highness, some of those arrested are proving helpful in revealing the motives, even the *misunderstandings* of some of the main conspirators. It leads me to ask your royal guidance.'

'I see. And would that guidance concern how they should be punished?'

'They are being helpful, as I said.'

All except Essex, both knew. He was reported to be veering wildly between belief in his exoneration at trial and consolation from religion against his impending death.

'Helpful?' the Queen asked, examining the word. 'I imagine they ought to be.'

'Your Highness is so often inclined to magnanimity.'

Elizabeth laughed.

'Woman's indecision, your father called it, when he was being polite.'

Her voice turned severe.

'I do not enjoy signing death warrants.'

Cecil knew it, as his father had before. How many times had Scots Mary conspired against her before she put the pen to the paper which struck off her head?

'Remember, little man, if the insurgents had won their way, I would not be here today listening to your advice and you would be where they are now, in the Tower, awaiting your own trial under their perversion of the law.'

Cecil gave a modest bow of understanding before speaking again.

'If Your Highness were to exercise clemency in cases where you are persuaded that no further threat will ensue, then I see no reason why mercy should not be recognised by ... substantial compensation.'

'You mean *fines*?'

Elizabeth's eyes glittered at the mention of money. It was a Tudor family trait.

'Fines, small fortunes, ransoms for their lives in line with the gravity of the offence,' Cecil said.

'God knows, the exchequer needs replenishing after what was wasted by My Lord Essex in Ireland,' the Queen replied, turning the proposition over in her mind.

A deeper regret appeared to interrupt her.

'Has there been any word from ... him, a request for pardon?'

The unspoken question. Cecil was brisk.

'Pardon can only be granted by the Crown. May I presume that he has not, not yet, approached Your Highness?'

Cecil was known to see every communication coming out of the Tower, permitted or illicit from any of the prisoners.

Elizabeth did not answer. A covert glance from Cecil to the lady-in-waiting received the reassurance he was seeking – there had been no leaks, the Queen had not yet been approached. So far as was known, Essex was still oscillating between deep despair at his fate and trust in vindication before his peers. Could he really not see that the result was never in doubt when the State went to the time, trouble and cost of public proceedings? No dance had an unplotted final measure.

'Little man,' the Queen warned him, the steel restored to her voice, 'do not shield me from any such appeal. I know my duty.'

The following morning found Palmer busying himself at the Bell Inn. He was looking for the Stratford carriers for the journey into Warwickshire. When they appeared, the landlord introduced Palmer to the older of the pair, a tall, lean figure who explained the arrangements.

'We travels by packhorse – roads too soft for wagons, wagons too hard for travellers. Thirty miles a day's the limit so it's a three-day run by way of Oxford. Stop-overs – High Wycombe, then one of the Cotswold towns depending on the weather we gets and the progress we makes.'

'What if I want to get on more quickly?' Palmer asked him.

William Greenaway appeared to give it a moment's thought.

'If we has gentleman travelling with us, they sometimes goes on ahead, having the right to carry arms and suchlike to protect theirselves. Fact is, yow might be lucky – we're expecting Mr John Lane and his son. He's had business in London to attend to on behalf of the Lord of the Manor in Stratford – Mr Lane's his man. Likes to get on if he can. Son's a bit wild, but Mr Lane knows the way. Takes half a day or so off the journey.'

Palmer settled terms, including the hire of a horse at the going rate of a shilling a day. He was given the time of departure, an hour before dawn on the next day, Wednesday.

Once Palmer had gone, Greenaway took the landlord aside.

'What's the man's story then? Says he's on legal business in Stratford. Don't dress like a lawyer,' Greenaway said.

'You can trust 'im.'

'Just as well.'

When the landlord caught up with Palmer, he tipped him off about his clothes.

'Lawyers never dresses poor,' he warned.

The Greenaway company rode out of the City in the breaking light of early morning, in the middle of them Richard Palmer chafing in a new suit of clothes on a horse he was unsure of.

They travelled through Newgate, towards Holborn and over the bridge across the Fleet river where the waters flowed fresh from the neighbouring countryside. At Holborn bridge the water changed its colour to murky-grey, stinking with sewage from the dense surrounding buildings. Palmer held his nose. Ten years in the city and he still resented its smell.

Soon they were free of it, heading west on the Oxford Road, past Tyburn Tree where the gallows stood. Its hangmen would soon be busy, Palmer reckoned as they rode by, thinking of the men locked away after Sunday's uproar.

'So, legal business in Stratford, is it?' Greenaway asked him.

'The name Shakespeare mean anything to you?'

'Shakespeares all round Stratford ... yow been called in by the Rowington Shakespeares? Hear they's got a row going on with their landlord.'

'My business is with the Shakespeares in Stratford town.'

Greenaway nodded in silent rumination.

'Only one family of that name in the town, old John, wife by the name of Mary, four sons and a daughter, neighbours of ours in Henley Street; all except the eldest, Will, moved into the big house on Chapel Street. Sound right?'

'Sounds right,' Palmer confirmed.

Greenaway appeared to weigh his passenger up, his face still obscure in the unclear light.

It stood to reason that a London lawyer might have business with London Shakespeare, Palmer was counting on. The Stratford man had done well for himself, he was 'Mr' now, gentleman, with plenty of money to invest. He was a man of means by every means. Such men had business with big town lawyers.

There was history between Greenaway's family and the Shakespeares which Palmer wasn't to know – threats of assault and court actions in the preceding generation. Not only that, but there was the old crack which ran deep in the town – religion, then and now. Mrs Greenaway was staunch for the old faith. Not that he was going to hear that from the man alongside him. William Greenaway was well-known in his home town for keeping his nose out of politics and religion. Some said the same about London Shakespeare. For him Greenaway ran errands up and down, the last a message from Shakespeare's family that old John his father wasn't well.

Palmer asked more about the Shakespeares.

'Family's split between two houses these days like I said,' Greenaway offered freely enough. 'Most lives in Henley Street, such as the old parents – they're still livin'- along with the daughter, married late, to a hatter, young family. '

When he was asked about William Shakespeare's standing in the town, Greenaway gave Palmer a sideways look before answering.

'Will's done well, bought the biggest house in town, New Place. Belonged to the Clopton family, 'im as was Lord Mayor of London they say and built the stone bridge over the river.'

'Big house?' Palmer asked.

'Yes, an' there's only the wife and the two girls, servants o' course. There has been tenants in there – can't rightly remember if they still be there.'

'No sons to inherit,' Palmer added with a nice touch of legal concern. He had heard as much from the actors.

'Nope. There was a boy but he died, the year before they moved in, five, six years back.'

'Chance of any more?'

'Only if God be willing and the wife can make miracles. Anne Shakespeare ain't young no more, ain't a well woman neither. The household's run by the elder daughter, a grown woman she be.....' Greenaway said and would have said more.

Instead he was interrupted by a voice from behind them, awkward and adolescent.

'Susanna Shakespeare! That stuck up piece of skirt!'

'Nick Lane,' Greenaway whispered to Palmer, son of the man who represented Stratford's Lord of the Manor.

The lad trotted his horse up alongside them.

'Too good for the likes of us Stratford lads, that's what *she* reckons,' he sneered. '*She* can read and *she* can write. *If* she marries it won't be to no ordinary Stratford lad, nor no gen'l'man unless he's educated. *My* father says a gen'l'man's born not made.'

Greenaway grinned at the boy's jibe at the Shakespeares' rise in the world.

'*And* she's a tartar for religion,' the boy complained, 'a nag in the home and a preacher outside it. But they're all the same under the skirts.'

'She's not for you then,' Palmer said.

'Her father's a common actor. That's what I tell her when she gets high and mighty. "No he's not,"' the boy mimicked her, '"he's a *hauthor*, his plays are performed at *court*."'

'Happens to be true.'

Palmer's remark made the boy spur his horse away from them. Good riddance, Palmer told himself.

'Bit wild, as I said,' Greenaway remarked, watching the boy ride on ahead, scattering rabbits and birds as he went. There was old trouble between the Lanes and the Shakespeares as well, had Palmer been bothered to enquire.

'Are the Lanes important people in Stratford?' Palmer asked the carrier.

'John Lane is the Lord of the Manor's man,' Greenaway contented himself with repeating as if that were enough.

Only when the party reached High Wycombe did Palmer and Lane senior exchange words. It was in the main room of the hostelry where they were staying.

'One of the best inns on the road,' John Lane said.

He gazed sombrely into his drink, a man, Palmer decided, who robbed you of your solitude without comforting your loneliness.

'I hear yow want to get ahead,' Lane said several minutes later. 'Greenaway told me. There's about fifteen miles of rising ground in front of us, well-forested, leading up to a ridge. Past that and we're down onto the Oxford plains. At that point, my boy and I reckon on cutting loose from our party.'

'What sort of time do you expect to make?' Palmer asked him.

'Tomorrow as far as Woodstock, a few miles beyond Oxford, maybe even Chipping Norton where we pick up the road which runs north by the river up to Stratford.'

'Well, it's true I need to make the best time I can,' Palmer admitted, at the same time not sure that a ride with the lugubrious Lane and his wild young son was worth it. Also, he was being hampered in his riding. He moved uncomfortably. It was an old trouble, an itching rash resurrected after years out of the saddle and irritated by his fresh-cut suit of clothes.

'I need to be sure I will get there by Friday morning.'

'We will be there by then.'

Palmer agreed to Lane's offer. Time saved was opportunity gained.

He decided to turn in early for the night, carrying with him a bowl of water to wash down the inflammation in the privacy of his chamber. As was about to go up, he caught sight of the Lane boy, his face flushed with drink. The servants were giving him a wide berth, the women particularly.

Something caused Palmer to hold back. Was it his imagination, or was there someone with the boy, on the other side of him like a shadow? Palmer looked again – no-one, only young Nick Lane with his hand on the backside of a serving girl who was trying to beat it away.

He laughed at himself for carrying his big city suspicions into the countryside.

In his room, he laid out the cache of sonnets on the bed and arranged lighted candles for reading. It was not a task he was looking forward to. He riffled through the pile of papers, reminding himself what he had collected so far – from Cecil's scavenging agents, a dozen verses prodding Southampton towards marriage; from the printed collection, a pair introducing the woman in the triangle; from Field maybe a hundred or more containing God knew what, and from Emilia a slim sheaf which he expected would contain love sonnets from the poet to her, but in whose cause?

Palmer went straight to those verses. The handwriting matched the Southampton presentation copies, the poet's own. The lover's suit was his own too. There was nothing so ridiculous to Palmer's mind than a lover out of character, in the wrong clothes.

'*My mistress when she walks treads on the ground.*'

Clever all the same to contrast her earthiness with the prevailing taste for virgin goddesses. But praise of her dark good looks soon changed into accusation.

'*So, now I have confessed that* he *is thine.*'

Palmer grabbed for the printed collection with the pair of poems marked by Cecil's chief official. He found the verse about the two loves, the better one 'a man right fair', the worse 'a woman coloured ill'. No prizes for guessing who the poet least wanted to lose, to his mind, and it wasn't the woman. Well, Southampton offered money and position. What had Emilia to offer beyond the pleasures of the bed?

He dragged the wad of sonnets taken from Field towards him. He found himself in a new world, of poet-mentor turned supplicant to a youth.

'*Then happy I, that love and am beloved.*'

Really?

His eyes fastened onto the next group of sonnets. From one to the next, they took the writer away from his friend, travelling. Themes of separation interplayed, like music by a writer conscious of material too good to waste, worth working up, repeating, adding variation. Morbidity entered the poet's voice, fear of premature death and the judgement of history that his art was unsophisticated. Since when did men write their own epitaphs, Palmer asked himself?

The writer's distance from his friend lent self-doubt.

'*Alas, he was but one hour mine.*'

In an extended trio, the poet forgave injury from his friend. Poet blamed woman, owning up to his greatest fear.

'… *that she hath* thee.'

The Emilia episode ended. The friend was once again resurrected:

'*thou best of dearest and mine only care.*'

Accusation re-entered the scene; his friend was letting himself down – putting himself around, Palmer wondered? – followed by a massive outpouring of self-pity.

'*No longer mourn for me when I am dead.*'

And then

'*Farewell, thou art too dear for my possessing.*'

Too dear by half!

A protracted exchange brought fresh agitation, the poet protesting his willingness to take all the blame and end the friendship. Disillusion stalked the verses, warning of the 'canker in the fragrant rose', arguing for continence, restraint, dignity.

In answer to Palmer's unspoken prayer, the sheets thinned to a final handful. A calming tone settled on them.

'*Take thou my oblation, poor but free,*
Which is not mixed with seconds, knows no art
But mutual render, only me for thee.'

Palmer yawned. The yawn masked another unease, that the connection between the muse and his poet went way beyond what he had been expecting. He leaned across to snuff out the bedside candles. Sleep would not come. Thoughts nagged him wide awake – about the sort of relationship which went far beyond master–servant and in explicit words. Case proved? Not yet. The sonnet story and any claim it had as written evidence had ended years ago. On the other hand, a man who could write such verses, such a man might be capable of anything at any time.

Sleep finally descended, but not the dreamless. Early in the morning he awoke from a nightmare, bathed in sweat, the sonnet sheets scattered from bed to floor.

~ 8 ~

THE NEW DAY brought better weather so that the breakaway group was able to make good time. Nick Lane was in his element, racing ahead in short, dust-stirring bursts while his father followed at a steadier rate. It was as much as Palmer could do to stay in touch given the slow–quick-slow rhythm of his place as the backmarker.

In Oxford they stopped to water the horses on the Broad, the widest street in the city. Palmer looked around him, at where martyrs had burned alive for their faith less than half a century before. Their beliefs were Protestant heresy then, State orthodoxy now. He heard in his head his father's unpitying judgement voice, that they had deserved what they received. How could men deserve death for speculating on what could not be proved or disproved? Ah, but ideas were the riskiest currency of all.

His body felt taut and tired, unused to the jolting of long riding. The inflammation was suppurating, he could feel it. All the same, he accepted the Lanes' determination to press on.

The older Lane was no more cheerful than the night before.

'See these roads,' he complained, 'they should be fifty feet across, and what would yow say they are? Half that! *And* going to rut and ruin!' It came as no surprise to Palmer to be told whose fault it was – 'it was the common folks!' – in not keeping the roads repaired.

They arrived in Chipping Norton as dark began to cloak the Cotswold hills. At the inn Palmer called for warm water to take up to his chamber, and this time, a little salt. The stink of his inflammation disgusted him. He winced as he applied the salted water to the broken skin. The prospect of the shorter ride to Stratford the following day did not appeal.

He went downstairs to eat and to sound out John Lane.

'Frankly, yowr business with Shakespeare is no business of mine,' Lane told him, eating quickly from the plates set before him and guzzling loudly from a base metal cup.' He and I are of an age. I don't like the trade he's in, it's not an employment for a respectable man but then,' he added, touching his mottled nose significantly, 'he's made money at it so he's Mr William Shakespeare *Gent* which is all very well but ... he needs to decide where he stands!'

Palmer asked him what he meant.

'Simple. Is he with the gentry, the class he now claims to belong to, or with the common folk which is, let's be frank, where he comes from. They're sticklers for their ancient rights, yowr common folk, but the land has to be made to pay.'

He touched his nose again to share a further confidence.

'Agriculture, we all know, is in a slump. Livestock is the way forward, needs fewer folk to mind it and that means closing in the fields and the common land, hedging and gating it. Oh but no, the locals say, we've always grazed our pig on the common.'

'And where does Shakespeare stand on this?' Palmer asked.

'Yow tell me.'

Lane's glance at Palmer was shrewd.

If Lane was typical of the Stratford sort, how a man must long for the peace and repose of London, was what Palmer was thinking.

The final ride to Stratford by way of Shipston through pelting rain, on a bony, winded nag was as grim as Palmer had feared. Water penetrated the collar of his cloak and ran down into his body chilling it worse than any dry cold could. His relief was heartfelt when he saw the bridge across the Avon to Stratford appear.

Clattering over it, down the causeway over marshy land on the northern side, Palmer picked out the sign of the Swan, the inn recommended to him by Lane as the best in town. Dismounting with Palmer, Lane introduced him to the landlady while his son trotted on in the direction of their home in Rother Street. She was quick to offer her mud-spattered guest warm water and a fire in a private chamber. As he went up, following a servant, Palmer heard only one of the words Lane and the landlady were exchanging in whispers – 'Shakespeare.'

In his chamber Palmer washed himself down. His infection was leaking blood as well as pus. Did the town boast a capable apothecary or doctor? He preferred the first; they were less lethal in his experience.

The landlord, when asked, was at first hard-pressed to give a decent answer.

'We've a new, youngish doctor in town, a university man they say, trained abroad,' he finally suggested, adding 'sound in his religion just the same', just so the stranger did not get the wrong idea.

Palmer showed interest.

'Name of Dr Hall, works over by the Church,' the landlord told him. 'If yow like, I'll send him word. He's a hard-working man by all accounts. He'll come out soon as he's free.'

The doctor looked older than his years in his severe black suit. His manner was confident, direct and relatively gentle. He required few preliminaries and his speech was free from gobbledygook, medical or astrological. It reassured his patient, Palmer.

'It's a mess,' he said after examining the infected area. From his bag he brought out clean lint and a salve to cleanse the wound. 'They call it a sweating rash,' Dr Hall explained. 'The riding, rubbing, sweat and rainwater have not helped. The salve will do for now, but it will help if you keep it dry and clean. How long are you staying in Stratford?'

A couple of days, Palmer told the doctor, who shook his head.

'It won't heal in that time.'

He asked Palmer more questions – had he suffered broken skin or abrasions on other parts of the body? Palmer admitted that he had, beginning in his soldiering days. The doctor nodded, taking the information in.

'You're an educated man, I would say, so you understand the basic regimen of the body, its humours – phlegm, bile, choler and so on? Good. Now it's only my opinion, but I have seen some men whose humour is manifested through the skin. Once agitated, it is made tender and irritated. If this tenderness is heated, wetted and abrased, inflammation follows. The skin breaks and that is when infection enters. The infection is the result, not the cause.'

The doctor was not finished.

'There is a compound I have found to be useful. If you call round to my house tomorrow...'

Hall gave his patient directions. He stated his fee, not country-cheap, Palmer felt, but fair if it led to a cure.

'The landlord told me you were new to the town,' Palmer said.

'I've been building up my practice here for a year or so. You were lucky to find me in. I'm frequently away, travelling to my patients.'

'Would those patients include the Shakespeares?'

It was a fair shot, Palmer reckoned – old John Shakespeare was reported ill and his son, the London gentleman, would surely want the best for his family.

The doctor's answer was curt.

'I do not disclose information on my medical practice,' he said. 'I will see you in the morning.'

The landlord was more forthcoming when Palmer went downstairs. He knew the Shakespeares well, he said – his father had trained John Shakespeare in the glovemaking trade fifty years before. He gave Palmer directions to New Place, the Shakespeare home.

'Yow can't miss it – opposite the Gild Chapel.'

His eyes appeared narrow within their jolly mask.

'Legal business, is it?'

Palmer hinted at business in London.

The landlord's eyes did not relax.

'Can't say as I've seen him of late,' he said – a lie, Palmer was sure. 'He's usually here at midsummer. Now tell me,' he said, changing the subject, 'what's all these rumours from London?'

Palmer slept like the dead and rose stiff but rested. The infection was easier. He washed and dressed it again before setting off into the town.

A man in a doorway opposite watched him go.

Palmer walked on, oblivious, towards the centre of the town, the man following him from the other side of the street. No-one passing them in the opposite direction offered any greeting to these two strangers in town.

Palmer stopped across the way from what he took, from the landlord's directions, to be New Place. He saw an imposing townhouse new a century before, boldly – and expensively – finished using brick between the timber frame in place of the more usual plaster. It impressed the investigator, boasting twenty yards of frontage, three storeys and five gables with windows to match. The old Palmer family home in Kent had been no bigger.

There was little sign of movement inside, no bustling for an early departure. So far so good, Palmer reckoned, slipping round the corner to check the side of the building. His tracker moved unseen in tandem with him.

Palmer found a porch-entrance built into a garden wall. He imagined a garden behind, maybe an orchard too. Leaving it, he wandered further down where he found barns among a cluster of elms. When he turned to retrace his way, his tracker slipped out of sight.

Palmer stopped at a halfway point to look over the property's enclosing wall. It revealed its secret. Set over a small lawn was a pretty manor house built in stone and brick with signs of recent work judging by the piles of unused materials in front of it.

So this was where the family lived; the frontage was no more than its public face. Such is the age, Palmer told himself with the envy of the dispossessed.

He walked back up the lane, past the Chapel on his left. Mr Shakespeare could wait for the time being, he decided. It was time for him to find his young physician. His mood was careless. He still had not noticed the cloaked figure continuing to follow him at a careful distance.

'I should purge you,' Dr Hall said in the working room of his house when Palmer was shown in.

There was no wife and family from what Palmer saw, only an elderly servant.

'How long would that take?' he asked.

'Five days or so.'

'Not possible, I have to leave town sooner, so, no purging; no bleeding either!'

'Bleeding would achieve nothing in your case,' Hall said. 'Used in moderation, it can be beneficial. However, a purge would be best. After that a herbal bath to promote sweating and then the application of the special ointment I recommended yesterday.'

'What's in the ointment?' Palmer asked, suspicious – if there was any mention of frogs or bats, he wasn't having it.

'Herbal ingredients – elecampane, briony, a little alum with butter to make the application smooth. You cleanse the infection daily then apply the ointment and it should begin to soothe the irritation after a day or two. Purging and sweating would get to the root of the problem, but if you say that you don't have time, then the ointment will help. Now, let me see how it is today.'

Palmer allowed himself to be examined.

'Better,' the doctor said, 'you have kept it clean and dry as I instructed. I take you to be a man of clean habits. You wash your body from time to time?'

Palmer nodded.

'A countryman then, or a man of good family.'

'Both,' Palmer agreed then asked the doctor where he came from – his accent was not the local sing-song sound.

'My father is a physician with a practice close to London. I came to Stratford to set up on my own. I learned a great deal from my father, but a man must strike out for himself.'

He was such an old, young man, Palmer couldn't help thinking. Where did women figure in the life of this paragon of medical virtue?

'I saw no mistress in the house when I came in.'

The doctor appeared to blush.

'A doctor is a doctor first and foremost, a professional man who must establish and maintain a good practice. If he wants, he can marry, but not before he is thirty. That is my settled view.'

In that moment he looked to Palmer innocent and embarrassed, a glimpse of the young man under the medical carapace. If he had ever been close to a woman's body, Palmer reckoned, it was only in the interests of medicine.

'Mr   Shakespeare   has   daughters,'   he   suggested mischievously.

Hall returned a vexed look.

'Many gentlemen have many daughters here in Stratford.'

'Of course, you don't know him, Mr Shakespeare that is, he is usually away.'

'You answer your own questions, Mr Palmer, now if you don't mind...'

'The daughters you would meet in church, old grandfather Shakespeare too.'

'John Shakespeare does not come to church, Mr Palmer.'

What did that mean? If the old man was ill it might explain it. There was something in the crispness of the doctor's answer which indicated a more serious state of affairs. It might mean recusancy, fines for avoiding the present rite of worship. Palmer shuddered – his own youth had been full of his father's fighting for his faith, doing them no good at all.

'As for Mr Shakespeare's wife and children,' Dr Hall said, 'I make it a point not to chatter in church. It is a house of prayer, not a market or a fair.'

He stood up to finish the consultation.

'Mr Palmer, what *is* your business here in Stratford?'

Palmer stood up to answer him.

'As you might say, Dr Hall, it would be wrong of me to disclose it.'

~ 9 ~

OUTSIDE, WHITE STEAM rising from the lungs of the men and beasts passing New Place mingled with the cold winter air of early morning. For the second time, Palmer stood opposite the house with a decision to make. He approached the front entrance on the main street.

The door was answered by a servant, just as he expected. He asked for Mr Shakespeare. The servant shook her head.

'Master's not here.'

Palmer asked for the mistress. A young woman came forward from out of the shadows.

'What is yowr business?'

It amused Palmer when young played old. Susanna Shakespeare's voice was firm but its gravity was weakened by a girlish tone.

'Business from London,' Palmer replied.

He expected her to give way. She did not, but looked him up and down. He was grateful for the landlord's advice in London. She would have turned him away out of hand in his old clothes.

'My father is not here.'

'Where might I find him?'

'He left town early this morning.'

'Oh yes?'

Palmer was worried. Had he come all this way only to miss his prize?

'For London?'

'Unless I know yowr business, sir, I cannot say. My father was not expecting anyone or he would have told me.'

She was nobody's fool.

'It's business to do with the Globe,' Palmer gambled.

She looked unsure.

'Come inside please,' she said at last.

They entered a large room where the household plainly received visitors. It was dominated by a long oak table, poorly lit but warmed by a healthy fire.

The young woman who ushered him in was not tall, Palmer judged, but neat and plainly dressed. Her hair was auburn, thick and parted in the middle, flowing out long at the back through her linen cap. The face was not strictly pretty – her nose was too long for that – but her looks carried, as men said. Palmer admired her eyes, well-shaped in a feline way, hazel in colour whenever the light coming in from outside caught them.

They were not alone. Palmer saw in the depths of the room an older woman sitting by the fire. This one was heavier in build with, despite her ageing looks, a fairer colouring than the girl. The woman did not seem to resent the intrusion. She appeared to Palmer to be waiting for eternity.

'My mother,' Susanna Shakespeare explained.

'I must speak to your father,' Palmer said.

'Yow did not give yowr name.'

Palmer gave it now.

'I have never heard my father mention yow. It is not a name I recognise.'

She was no pushover, Palmer realised, this juvenile mistress of the house with a mother to care for and a father away for most of the time. The Globe ruse had got him through the door but it wouldn't get him much further.

'You've heard the news from London?' he tested her, unsure if she had.

'Rumours,' she said.

They had sickened her, coming hard on the heels of her father's surprise return from London. The names associated with the rumours – Essex, Southampton – did little to calm her. They were men she felt she knew conjured up out of tales her father used to tell her about their fine looks and rich costumes, the brilliance of their company and the magnificence of their palaces.

'And will I marry one like them?' she had once asked him when she was too young to know better, only to see his eyes cloud over with regret.

He was part of their world, he used to mean in the days when he talked about such things. It was so exciting – why ever should her mother want him to come home to the life of the fathers of her friends – the tanners and the butchers, the bakers and the other shopkeepers? He was beyond them now and if he was, then so was she!

'They've closed the Globe and all the playhouses,' Palmer said, bringing her back to the present. 'The actors are out of work.'

'Yow're not an actor.'

'Not an actor, no, but I am one of the Lord Chamberlain's household. He has the best interests of his actors at heart but the situation is serious. There may be ways and means he can help, only his Lordship needs to confer with all the leading men including your father, which is why I have been sent here after him.'

He watched the effect of the plausible lie and the softening of her attitude to him.

Susanna was relieved that the problem appeared to be one of work and nothing to do with the stories already circulating in Stratford, of violence and rebellion on London streets. Whatever fancy had led her mind into fearing that the actors were mixed up in that?

An agitated rapping at the door interrupted them, followed by the sound of an excited female voice in the doorway.

'Miss Susanna, it's yowr Grandad – he's having another one of his fits!'

They found the old man staring ahead at no fixed object, placed like an immoveable object in his chair in the parlour of the house on the other side of town. Palmer was with them, determined not to lose contact with the girl, offering a man's help.

The worried woman standing over the old man was, Palmer guessed, Shakespeare's sister. She had the same dark colouring as her niece. Opposite them, in the only other chair in the room sat an old woman, gaunt-faced, white-haired, rigidly controlling her anger.

Palmer argued for sending for Dr Hall.

'I've had reason to use him myself,' he said to Susanna.

A servant was sent for the new doctor.

'He tried to kill me again!'

Sharp and firm, the complaint came from the old woman. No-one spoke. From the back of the house a young child was crying. She couldn't mean Dr Hall surely, Palmer told himself. If she did, it was quick work even by a doctor's standards!

'What happened, Aunt Joan,' Susanna asked.

'Oh, I don't rightly know.'

The woman was flustered, the baby continued to cry.

'I think Father and Mother had words, leastwise Mother did. I came in and found him halfway across the room, eyes blazin', fist raised. Then he collapses on the floor. It was as much as we could do, Mother and me, to get him back into his chair. It's not the first time neither.'

'I told yow, he was going to kill me,' the old woman insisted.

'Yow weren't, were yow Grandad.'

Susanna's statement produced an even more truculent look on the old man's face. His mouth worked but nothing came out. He waved a hand in disgust at his own incapacity.

'Oh yes, he was,' Mary Shakespeare said. 'And you needn't sit there pretending yow can't talk. Yow've got words enough for me when you want, always did have.'

An awkward silence was broken by a knock at the door. Dr Hall came in. He looked at the old couple, sizing up the situation.

'Please leave me with the patient,' he said as kindly as his nature allowed.

Mary Shakespeare resisted.

'I'm his wife!' she protested.

With his eyes the doctor signified that the women should help her away into the kitchen. He began a thorough examination of the old man.

'He's not been well for the best part of a year,' Susanna explained. 'It was all so sudden. One day he was his usual self, next day he wasn't making any sense, his wits were all over the place. We put him to bed, had him bled, purged and dosed, but it didn't help. Now he can barely speak. And he keeps having these fits.'

'He's got words enough for me when he wants,' the old woman shouted from the kitchen, 'and if he's poorly, he's only got himself to blame.'

Susanna blushed in embarrassment.

'It's a judgement on his ungodliness, when he wandered from the path,' Mary Shakespeare added before a door was closed on her.

Dr Hall took the young woman aside. Palmer pretended not to hear the low-voiced diagnosis. When it ended, the doctor turned to leave, expecting Palmer to follow him. Palmer stood his ground. His business was unfinished, he wanted an answer to where William Shakespeare was.

'But I have to look after my grandfather,' Susanna said wearily.

'You know I have to see your father.'

He felt Dr Hall's unlikely arm go round his shoulders.

'Now is not the time,' the doctor said. 'We must leave the family to get on.'

'I will call on you later,' Palmer called out to Susanna Shakespeare as he went. 'I will want an answer.'

Outside on the other side of the road, a stranger backed away into shadows as the door of the house opened. Palmer and Hall walked in silence up Henley Street towards the centre of town.

The doctor spoke first.

'Are the Shakespeares in trouble, Mr Palmer?'

Palmer ignored the question.

'Tell me about the old man,' he asked instead.

'Are you interested in medical matters, Mr Palmer?'

Palmer's first impulse was to deny it. Instead he mumbled what might have been taken for a yes.

'Contrary to what I suspect you believe, Mr Palmer, we doctors do not know everything, only God does. A good doctor must do what he can. Equally, he must be prepared to say when he cannot help as much as when he can.'

'You think the old man's incurable?'

'He's past seventy. There are few enough his age in this town. He must have been born in the time of old King Henry, he's lived through Edward and Mary and now Elizabeth. Believe me, Mr Palmer, the confused often revert to childhood. They babble, they dribble, they forget their own names, their age, they mistake their daughters for their wives.'

'But not this man.'

'No, he knows his own thoughts. What he has lost is his power to express them. I checked for bodily signs of apoplexy, what some call a stroke, and there was none. One might argue that while the mind can think, the mouth cannot express due to some break in the chain. We do not know enough about the subject.'

A doctor confessing ignorance was new to Palmer.

'So what can you do?'

'The man is old, I cannot give him back his youth. In my experience, old men do not fully recover from such conditions so that all that we can do is soften them. He doesn't sleep well. I can give him something for that. There are the usual aches and pains of old age. I have medicaments which may ease them. As for his illness, the only treatment is peace.'

'Is that likely to happen? You heard his wife!'

'She is frightened, Mr Palmer. We lash out against what we do not understand. Maybe she can be brought to understand, only time will tell.'

The doctor held out his hand for Palmer to shake. Palmer took it then watched him go.

A voice from behind interrupted him.

'See yow've met out God-bothering doctor.'

Palmer turned to find the bumptious Nick Lane. He decided to move off.

'Found yowr man yet?' the boy shouted after him. 'Old Shakespeare's son?'

It stopped Palmer in his tracks.

'No,' he said, turning round.

'Not surprising, that.'

'Why?'

'He's not here.'

Palmer turned back to the boy.

'So where is he then?'

The boy danced from one foot to another.

'Father sent me to tell yow. One of my father's men saw him out riding.'

'Who?'

'Master Shakespeare, Master William.'

'Riding where?'

'He wasn't riding at the time. He was standing.'

Palmer put his face close to the boy's who jumped back, laughing.

'By the church,' he said. 'Not the church here,' the boy taunted him.

'Where, for Christ's sake?'

A couple of housewives scurried past, frightened by the language.

'Snitterfield. It's a village, four miles out of town on the Warwick road.'

'*Thank* you,' Palmer said with elaborate sarcasm, still unsure whether to believe him, 'how can I ever repay you?'

The young man began to hop from one foot to another again. There was something he wanted.

'Put in a word for me with Susanna? I saw yow with her just now.'

'Ha! You'll get no fal-lal-lal with her, young man.'

~ 10 ~

PALMER CURSED the lost time as he flogged himself on foot along the road to Snitterfield. Was he going on a wild goose chase? His limbs were still aching from the long ride from London, the unsoftened wool of his new suit was rubbing against the rawness in his groin, his boots stumbled in and out of frozen cart ruts. He felt miserable but the old soldier in him kept him going. He had seen and been in far worse, or so he regularly reminded himself.

Looking up from time to time, the hedgerows on either side appeared barren to him except for an evergreen here and there. Birds were silent. A steady drizzle turned into light snow gusting into his face with each blast of a wind which was blowing up, always up the road. Christ, how he hated the country in winter even more than the city in summer. He was alone on the road with nothing ahead of him. Or was he? For a moment he could swear he'd had a sight of a horse and rider in the snowblinding haze ahead. Soldiers talked of such phantom things seen in battle. To him, they were just an illusion.

A walk of an hour took him half as long again in the conditions, past a broad park on the right which he barely acknowledged what with his head held down against the elements. No traffic came in the opposite direction. If the boy was right about where Shakespeare was, he had to come back this way which should mean that he was still there.

At last Palmer came to a straggle of homes heralding a village, unusually spread out. Pressing on, he saw the outline of a church through the wind and snow, ahead of him to his right. It was large for a village's needs, announcing itself with a staunch, squat tower. He headed for its porch.

A man hidden from sight in a snow-covered copse watched him go in. He pulled a pair of firearms from the saddle of his horse.

The interior of the church was dark, its candles left unlit. Palmer stepped gingerly through an arcade of arches past an ancient font. What little light existed struggled through the high clerestory windows. When his eyes adjusted, the church appeared deserted. Had the boy lied?

He stopped to listen. He thought he heard a noise, from behind another door on the opposite wall. He crossed the nave towards it, pausing outside. Inside he heard movement.

He pushed open the door without knocking. A welcome rush of warm air hit his body from a lighted brazier in the corner. A man had his back to him, head stooped over papers he was studying. The man spoke without looking round.

'Welcome at last, cousin.'

It was a businesslike voice in the mood for deal making.

Palmer said nothing. The man fitted the description, that was all.

Shakespeare turned round. For a second he stared at the incomer before falling back in surprise. Palmer saw the man's eyes dart surreptitiously to his belt looking for weapons. Palmer raised his arms to show that he was unarmed. His quarry's eyes shifted around the room, looking for exit.

With an easy foot, Palmer felt for the dagger in his boot. He wouldn't need it, he judged. Shakespeare looked lean and fit but unarmed – easier to hit him once and hard than try to restrain him. He saw with satisfaction that the door behind the man was barred.

'Who are you?' Shakespeare asked. There was fear in his voice which the actor in him was trying to mask.

'Who were you expecting, Mr Shakespeare?' Palmer asked him, unaware of cousins and property deals and legacies to be reclaimed.

'It doesn't matter,' Shakespeare said.

Palmer looked him over more carefully. The resemblance to the daughter was unmistakeable – the same eyes and cast of face, the rich brown hair, thick at the sides if thin on the crown and in the beard. There was no doubt he had found his man.

'My name,' he announced, 'is Richard Palmer. I have a commission from the Chief Minister to find you, question you in respect of the performance of the King Richard play on February 7th this year – a week ago today – and its relation to the uprising led by the Earls of Essex and Southampton and then conduct you to London to await the Crown's pleasure.'

As commissions go, it was the most impressive Palmer had ever had. He enjoyed rehearsing it.

'And your written authority?' Shakespeare demanded.

Palmer remembered what Lambarde had told him – the playwright knew his law. He pulled out the warrant Cecil had given him.

Shakespeare came closer in order to read it while Palmer held it up between them so that he could see it in the flickering light provided by the brazier. If there was any trouble he would threaten to hand the man over to the local magistrates. They would be keen to show their worth to Whitehall when the State was in jeopardy.

'If you want any more paper, I can give you plenty, ' Palmer said, 'reams of sonnets, written to a man arrested for treason; sonnets recovered from a traitor's lodgings with useful additions from your publisher and an old bedmate. A bookful of sonnets!'

Shakespeare's eyes dropped. He turned to fold away his papers.

The two men walked out through the porch into the harsh winter weather. Shakespeare began unhitching his horse.

From across the way the man in hiding levelled the long barrel of a horse pistol towards them.

Palmer thought he heard a click, an inconsequential sound to anyone other than a soldier. He fought off the instinct to freeze. His eyes darted to where he thought the sound came from but no, he must be imagining it. He was getting too old for this sort of thing, he reflected, moving forward to stop his prisoner who was in the action of mounting up. He looked around about them once again. Nothing moved, beyond wind on trees and bushes shaking out a shimmering of snow.

The two men walked on their way, leading the single horse as if nothing had happened.

They struggled through the gusting snow, on their way back to Stratford. It was neither the time nor the weather to talk.

They arrived back in town in the early afternoon, stopping first at the Henley Street house. Palmer accompanied Shakespeare in.

'I must go back to London,' Shakespeare told his father in the parlour, clasping the old man's hands in his.

Anxiety showed in the old man's eyes, whether for his son or for himself Palmer did not care to guess. He had no feelings for the victims of his trade – justice was a matter for others, not for him, or so he told himself.

Shakespeare repeated his message to his mother and his sister in the kitchen. The sister cried. The old woman was stronger, signing the old, forbidden blessing of the cross on her son's forehead.

Across at New Place, Shakespeare gave orders for two fresh horses to be ready for the ride to London next morning. In the house he was met by Susanna, agitated and anxious.

'There's been a stranger from London asking after yow. And Grandad has had one of his turns!'

She stopped stock still when she saw Palmer. Her father kissed her forehead, his first act of tenderness towards her since his return.

'I know,' he consoled her. 'Mr Palmer has important news. He came to find me to tell me.'

'But I didn't...'

Shakespeare's hand soothed her forehead.

He asked Susanna about her mother. From the girl's reaction it was clear that she was no different. With a gesture to Palmer, Shakespeare excused himself to speak to her.

He found her in her sanctuary, the kitchen.

'I have to return to London,' Palmer heard him say to her from where he lurked in the doorway.

She appeared to show only dull acceptance. She might think differently, Palmer reckoned, if she knew it was the last time. Was he a good husband? Palmer pushed such softness from his mind.

'I've left plenty of money,' Shakespeare told her.

She gave him a pale smile of thanks as if to please him.

He touched her hands. She looked up at him with wounded eyes.

'I hate,' she said, 'not yow.'

It seemed to mean something between them. Her husband smiled and then kissed her.

The room where Shakespeare took Palmer was a place of work rather than comfort. The largest article of furniture was a country-made bed.

'You said you had sonnets of mine,' Shakespeare said.

'They tell an interesting story,' Palmer replied, 'the story of a man and his muse and a woman who came between them.'

'Do you think so? What if I said that they were no more than poetic imaginings?'

'And Catullus invented his Lesbia! Your friend and publisher Richard Field, when I interviewed him, he linked the sonnets with Southampton. So let's agree that Southampton was your patron and the sonnets' beating heart.'

Beating heart? He'd been reading too many sonnets, Palmer warned himself.

Shakespeare said nothing back.

Palmer attacked again.

'Two books of verse dedicated to a young star of the nobility, two of your *private* sonnets published two years ago, his attendance at your plays as recently as last year, they all tell an unbroken story up to the present time.'

About what, the look on the other man's face appeared to say?

'It was to *your* company the rebels turned when they were planning their crime, to *your* play about the removal of a reigning monarch by a popular candidate, a candidate Essex specially identified with.'

It was true, Essex liked dedications from apologist historians extolling the virtues of Henry Bolingbroke.

So what was he accused of, the mute appeared to be asking all the same?

'It's for the authorities to decide the charge,' Palmer said. 'As far as I'm concerned, I can show motive for your complicity and back it up with evidence.'

He felt Shakespeare's eyes examining him.

'For God's sake!' Palmer cursed then calmed himself down, lowering his voice. 'The play was deliberately put on the day before an armed revolt, paid for by the insurgents themselves. Or were they out for an afternoon's pleasure?'

Silence.

Palmer altered his line of questioning.

'Let's talk about the sonnets. My guess is that there are more, and if there are, you'll have them here. I have those kept by Field and some from a woman – Emilia Bassano is the name you would remember her by.'

Shakespeare did not appear to flinch.

'I could of course send a messenger to the magistrates asking for them to authorise search and discovery. That would mean turning your house upside down, disturbing your family and drawing the attention of half the town to your predicament.'

It was the type of threat which usually worked. It had with this man's publisher in London.

Shakespeare stood up. He went across the room to an iron-banded trunk. Pulling out a key from inside his shirt, he opened it. He retrieved a sheaf of papers, bringing them back to Palmer.

'You have nothing to say?' Palmer asked.

Shakespeare spoke at last.

'I like to keep my words for my work,' he said.

~ 11 ~

BACK AT THE SWAN, when Palmer was told that John Lane was here to see him, he was almost pleased to see him after the strange encounter with William Shakespeare. He was less happy about the boy Nick who accompanied him, or the hovering presence of the landlord behind. There were too many of them for comfort in the inglenook where he had chosen to dine.

Lane got to the point.

'We've put two and two together, Mr Palmer.'

Palmer resisted a joke.

'... we don't think yow are who yow say yow are.'

Palmer toyed with his food.

'Yow're no lawyer.'

'So what am I?' Palmer asked, looking up.

'An informer.'

'Oh really?'

'Of a sort. A bounty hunter.'

'So let me see, I'm in pursuit of William Shakespeare – for what? Writing bad plays?'

'No, for keeping bad company.'

'Care to tell me who? I might learn something.'

'We don't know precisely. Our guess is that it's to with the trouble in London. We hear as how Will was close to those locked up in the Tower for treason.'

'So, you are here to plead the case for this local lad led astray by his betters!'

Lane grinned at this, a slow wolf-like grin.

'I think yow mistake us for do-gooders, Mr Palmer.'

'Then let me guess,' Palmer said,' you want to *help* me in my task, in return for what? A little dropsie? A share in his property when the powers-that- be dismember his estate?'

The Palmers had known all about that.

'Like I said, Mr Palmer, we're not do-gooders. What yow've just said, you see, we can have that anyway. I'm the Lord of the Manor's man.'

'And so?'

Lane leaned forward into Palmer's face.

'The fact is, Shakespeare's *ours*!'

Palmer held the man's gaze despite the stink of his breath.

'So, you want a share of the bounty?'

The landlord spoke up from behind Lane.

'More'n that.'

'We believe that Master Shakespeare should be taken into *our* care,' Lane said, 'on behalf of the Lord of the Manor so that he can be taken before the magistrates.'

'I see. And what if I'm not a bounty hunter at all. What if I'm ... a Government agent?'

Lane did not appear surprised.

'This is Stratford, Mr Palmer, other writs run here.'

Palmer began to foresee the worst – a warrant might be lost, a man like him might disappear or be killed resisting arrest. What did it matter if the Government got its man? Who in Government cared who took the reward? He played for time.

'So, what's in it for me?'

'We're not do-gooders, Mr Palmer, I thought we'd explained.'

'I see.'

Palmer's left hand slipped down behind the table where he was eating, easing towards his boot. The moment Lane's eyes left him, in that split second he punched with his right deep into Lane's groin. As the man doubled up in agony, he swivelled him round and put the concealed blade to his throat.

'I *will* use it,' he warned. 'Boy! Get upstairs and bring down my saddlebags. Take more than a minute and your Dad will be coughing out his life blood!'

Palmer made a threatening movement towards John Lane's throat. The boy scuttled away to do as he was told.

'As for you, landlord, I shan't need your lodging tonight.'

The boy soon came back in with his bags. Palmer got him to throw them over. He picked them up with his free hand, his eyes never leaving the men opposite.

'Now, gentlemen,' Palmer said, easing himself and his hostage towards the door, 'I shall be staying elsewhere tonight. Mr Lane here will walk with me on my way and should there be any further *interruption* as we go, then Mr Lane here will meet his Maker before I do. Is that clear?'

The other two nodded.

'I am, as it happens, a Government man – I shouldn't trust what Mr Lane here thinks, not if I were you.'

Palmer began to force his hostage out of the little room and then out of the inn – Lane wasn't the first man he'd marched at knifepoint. Together they made the walk to Shakespeare's house, Palmer's one hand on Lane's shoulder, his hand holding a knife against his back.

'I'll still come after yow,' Lane wheezed as they approached the entrance to New Place.

Palmer swung him round and held the knifeblade to his gut.

'Just try!'

Then he threw Lane away into the night.

He kept his back to the door of New Place as he knocked repeatedly on it. It was answered by the Shakespeare girl.

'I've decided to accept your father's offer of hospitality,' Palmer announced. It was a lie but how could she deny him?

Palmer could not sleep. He didn't even try.

Instead he set about the tedious candlelit task of comparing the two collections of sonnets in order to discover any new ones. A quick count showed another forty or more needing to be read.

So he began. Some were variations on episodes already read, dedicated to the bitterness of complaint. Were they the most private of them all? Were they in fact unsent? The new ones were written on papers of different size and quality, in varying strengths of ink blotted, stained and scratched through. Some were lighthearted. The boy-muse had...

> '*A woman's face...*
> *A woman's gentle heart...*
> *An eye more bright than they...*
> *And for a woman wert thou first created.*'

Dangerous, flirty stuff, Palmer thought.

> '*But since she* pricked *thee out for women's pleasure,*
> *Mine be their love and thy love's use their treasure.*'

A disclaimer, Palmer wondered, or a come-on?

Familiar strains of self-pity emerged. Did the other party return that love? Or did Southampton leave his poet dangling? It wasn't up to him, Palmer decided, morality he left to others.

He came to the section on the dark woman, initially gallant, quickly turning sour. A new sonnet slowed his attention.

'The expense of spirit in a waste of shame
Is lust in action; and till action, lust
Is perjured, murderous, bloody, full of blame,
Savage, extreme, rude, cruel, not to trust,
Enjoyed no sooner but despised straight,
Past reason hunted, and no sooner had
Past reason hated...'

Such a volley of disgust could never have been sent. It made Palmer think of his own sterile encounter with Emilia Lanier, late payment for first love betrayed. He shook the sensation off. Men of his sort could not go in for self-examination.

~ 12 ~

THE KNOCK ON THE DOOR came early in the morning while it was still dark. It was a woman's tap by the soft sound of it, a maidservant with breakfast and water to wash with if he was lucky.

Palmer was surprised when the opening door revealed Susanna. She was carrying a tray. She did not turn to go as he expected.

'What will happen to my father?' she asked.

Palmer was unsure what to say. Shakespeare would have told her nothing was his bet. He eschewed what he was used to saying to wives hanging onto husbands under arrest, or to children weeping in the middle of one of life's nasty little dramas; his own defence against all the tawdry emotions from which he sought to cut himself off. He'd had enough troubles of his own.

'Your family will be all right,' was the single lie he could manage today.

'What do yow care once yow've done ... whatever yow call yowr job? What *will* happen to him?' she insisted, her voice close to breaking.

Interrogation, torture, locked away forever if he was lucky, taken out, strung up and carved in pieces if he wasn't; and his wife and children thrown on the street by the majesty of the law if there was profit for men like Lane to strip from the carcass of a family's fortune and misfortune. He knew something of it from his own family experience; but sympathy would change nothing for the girl in front of him.

He did the only thing in his power. He took the tray from the girl's shaking hands.

Down in the courtyard later in the morning, Palmer watched from a distance as a family group said their goodbyes by the lawn in front of the house. He busied himself checking his horse's harness. Loading the beast up, he looked up to the sky – the weather promised to be foul.

It was a larger gathering than he had seen before. In addition to Susanna – calmer than before or putting a brave face on it – there was a younger daughter with blonde country looks more like her mother's. Next to her, Palmer recognised Shakespeare's sister Joan accompanied by a tradesman-type he took to be her husband. In the doorway Shakespeare's wife stood fretting her hands. The old folk were absent.

'Is the ointment helping?'

It was the voice of Dr Hall.

'Feels more comfortable.' Palmer admitted. 'The ride today won't help.'

'... the body or the soul. Today is the Sabbath, Mr Palmer.'

Hall walked by towards the people gathered around the doorway. He acknowledged Susanna who introduced him to her father. Was it business or pleasure, Palmer wondered, which brought the doctor here? Shakespeare motioned him towards his wife. Perhaps it was a bit of both.

'Shouldn't be doing business on the Sabbath either,' Palmer said cheerily when the doctor walked back past.

Palmer and his prisoner rode their horses at walking pace out of the town.

Outside the Swan Inn, young Nicholas Lane was watching them go. Palmer's hackles rose again. Just annoyance at the boy, he told himself. Was he spotting for his father, the would-be arrester?

The great stone bridge ahead beckoned. As they crossed it, a light, wintry drizzle began to fall. Welcome to the joys of travel out of season!

Over on the other side, Shakespeare turned round in his saddle. Palmer knew what would be on his mind – would he ever see home again? Palmer wouldn't bet on it. He kept silent. It was an old technique. Soon the prisoner had to say something and that would get him talking.

Stratford disappeared behind them. Shakespeare remained silent. More miles accumulated under the horses' hooves. The rain started to penetrate the riders' cloaks and soak their caps.

Then it came.

'*We are the Earl of Warwick's men...*'

A lusty marching song began to batter the midwinter air.

Palmer pulled his head further into his cloak.

'*... and proud of our good name!*'

A wild whoop of laughter attached itself. Shakespeare turned in his saddle to his audience of one. Palmer let his prisoner talk.

'Doggerel isn't it? We sang it when we went down to London, in Armada-time.'

And so? Palmer said nothing. His prisoner turned halfway back and then stopped himself.

'There were six hundred of us, drilled hard so we could march down this road in proper military order. We marched in column of four, in step, our pikes shouldered. The company song kept our minds off our sore feet.'

Another explosion of the man's laughter made Palmer grit his teeth.

Another pause. Another attempt.

'We were all sorts because of the urgency of the time – green lads in the main, some old sweats who'd seen it all before – red-faced men with bottle noses, moaners against every form of authority. Our commander, now there was a haystack of a man, he told fantastic tales to make made your hair stand on end.'

'How did you get caught for duty?' Palmer asked him, a small first step in drawing the man in.

'Trouble with the magistrates. I was given the choice, lock-up, or your Queen needs you.'

Palmer wouldn't have thought he was the type to get into trouble. Then again, he was an actor and he was in trouble now.

'I was happy to go,' Shakespeare said. 'I substituted for another man – not that I got any money from it; that went to the recruiting officer.'

The same had been true for Palmer. Anything had to be better than dusty law books and the dry, probing questions of William Lambarde to an unwilling pupil who had not done his homework.

'I take it that you disapprove of plays, Mr Palmer.'

No he didn't, only modern ones with no understanding of classical principles. Palmer said as much. Shakespeare laughed again, that strange whoop.

'Ha! I see, the famous unities! Are you a student of history, Mr Palmer? Livy, Plutarch...'

'Caesar, Tacitus, Suetonius,' Palmer interrupted him to make a point.

'Ah, good. How about old Homer's Iliad?'

Yes, him too, Palmer replied through a laconic smile.

'The old poets, they all select their stories, drawing out the matter of interest, isn't that so? They don't tell them minute by minute, or day by day or just within a day. If they did, there wouldn't be a library big enough to hold them, would there?'

'I didn't make the rule,' Palmer said. 'Blame Aristotle.'

'So you follow rules, Mr Palmer. I had you down for a man who believes in little or nothing. And yet the arbitrary rules of ancient drama command your loyalty.'

Now it was Palmer's turn to stay silent.

'How would you write a play, say, about the Trojan Wars?' Shakespeare challenged him.

Palmer didn't bother to answer. It was obvious – he wouldn't, there were already enough epic poems by old masters of the craft. Who needed any more?

'You couldn't set it inside a day.'

'All right,' Palmer conceded, as if playing a game with a bored child on a long journey. 'The Trojan Wars. Where do you start?'

'We go directly into the action. We find the most dramatic moment in the story, its turning point.'

'The sack of Troy? Beginning with the Trojan horse taken into the city walls?'

'That's an end, not a beginning, and there's no ground for human quandary. The stage has moved on, Mr Palmer, scenes of war, pathetic as they are in the playhouse are no more than an incident or an illustration in the drama, they are no longer its heart. No, I say that the turning point is the death of Hector, Troy's champion, slain by dread Achilles. So, we leap over the beginnings of the War and we find the turning point, if only sulking Achilles can be drawn from his tent to serve his destiny and overthrow mighty Hector. Now, why would he?'

'We know why. Out of honour, to avenge the death of his bosom friend Patroclus.'

Talking of bosom friends ... but Shakespeare was not to be distracted from his subject.

'No, no, no, that's what Homer was paid to say by kings wanting the legends of their ancestors nobly painted. It's not how it really was, was it, Mr Palmer? It's not how it ever is. You know that. I know I don't insult you if I say your work is without honour. No, Hector fought because he had no other choice. Paris and Helen were parasites...'

'And Achilles?'

'A bully-boy, no better than Agamemnon, Menelaus, Ajax and the rest of them. We'll have him kill Hector in a cowardly ambush. Isn't that how it really goes?'

Palmer was inclined to agree without admitting it. He had seen little or nothing in war which could be described as honourable. Fear, boredom, excitement and squalor, yes, but little in the way of honour.

'Achilles is how we are, not how we want to be,' he heard his prisoner say. 'Ulysses now, he's the politician forced to do the dirty work while Nestor's an old bore, forever babbling on about a never-was golden past.'

Lambarde would love it, Palmer privately conceded. Cecil might not.

'... oh, we'll have to have a young couple at the heart of it – the public demands it – a couple with a foot in both camps, a touch of Romeo and Juliet which they'll lap up, only these young lovers will be no better than they should be either!'

They rode on into a brightening day. Palmer switched his mind from classical antiquity to lodgings for the night.

A blast of voice alongside him shocked him back into the present.

'*We march to meet the enemy*
And beat the King of Spain!'

A silence mercifully settled between the two men. Palmer began to doze in the saddle, kept awake only by the milder itching in his rump.

A flash from somewhere to his left dazzled him awake before his brain could catch up and he heard the report of the gun. His hat was gone and his staid old mare was rearing up in alarm. He battled to bring her under control.

'Robbers!'

The shout came from Shakespeare.

Palmer's old training kicked in – take off or take cover. It drilled him into action, his brain working at speed – a single shot not followed by another, a single attacker, having to reload...

He drove his horse forward towards the sound of the shot. He leaned low to present the smallest target. He saw a second flash from the copse ahead, without a crack of sound – misfire!

Horse and rider crashed through the undergrowth. Ahead of him Palmer saw the rump of the attacker's horse pumping, the arms of its rider frenziedly whipping up the reins in a desperate effort to escape. With the advantage of momentum, Palmer prepared to stab with his knife to bring the man down. He saw a glimpse of a face turned back towards him in panic. He stood up in the stirrups, then, without warning he felt himself being pitched forward, thrown half over the head of his horse which stumbled beneath him. He struggled to regain his seat while his mare limped to a hobbled walk – it must have misfooted into a pothole.

The thud of horse hooves galloping away across open country soon began to fade. Palmer stroked his horse's neck, both drinking in draughts of freezing air. This was no vicious accident of the road – robbers worked in numbers. His mind turned immediately to Lane and his accomplices. The top of his head felt cold. He dismounted and walked his horse back to the road.

Where was Shakespeare?

He looked up and down the road. Gone!

So, it was a set up.

There was nothing he could do, his own horse was lame. Should he walk it onto Oxford? No, too much time lost. It would be quicker to go back to the last town and hire a fresh horse.

He began to walk his horse back down the road, pausing to pick up his hat. A bullet hole was drilled neatly through the crown. Not a professional, a professional would have shot at the body to force him out of the saddle before finishing him off. What would he tell Cecil? No, it hadn't come to that, he must recapture his prisoner.

Excuses to a man like Cecil were a waste of time.

~ 13 ~

 I T WAS WELL into the night by the time Palmer reached Oxford on a new mount. He had lost half a winter day's light on his escaped prisoner. He made a rapid check on all the hiring points for fresh horses. He used Cecil's authority to get responses. There was no report of anyone matching Shakespeare's description.

He must have ridden on, Palmer decided. But where to? Back to Stratford by some circuitous road? No, there were plenty there who would turn his man in soon as look at him and he must know it. Would he head somewhere other than London? If he did, there was nothing Palmer could do about it.

Should *he* make a run for it as well? It was a persisting thought – he had good money in his purse. Yes, but for how long with a warrant out for his arrest with every sheriff in the land? No, better to do what he knew, go where he knew. The same must be true for his escaped prisoner, Palmer reasoned. Stick to the chase and there was a chance he would find his man again.

So, London.

In London a man could hide or find a ship to the continent. God knows, undercover Jesuit priests penetrated the capital like a sieve when they needed to. Suspects went to ground there and were never found. It would be a game of cat and mouse in a very large house.

He rode on through the night.

At High Wycombe Palmer was in luck – a man answering Shakespeare's description had changed horses there.

'How long ago?' he asked.

Half a day, he was told.

Shakespeare would be in London by now.

Palmer took another horse and used the ride to the capital to order his thoughts until clusters of houses turned into suburbs and they in turn gave way to the walls of the great City.

It was approaching Monday evening and the treason trial was due for Thursday. If Cecil expected to hear from him by Wednesday at the latest, it gave Palmer a day and two nights. What to do? Put the word round the inns and alehouses. Mark the cards of those Shakespeare might turn to – the actors and his former publisher Field. Shakespeare would want his money – the goldsmiths of Cheapside were the likely holders. The actors could tell him which one.

It was the beginning of a plan.

He did his round of the London drinking establishments that evening. At the Bell, he left extra word for the Greenaways, due up the following day.

'Tell them it's worth their while if they hear anything from friend Shakespeare to let me know – tell them it's Government business, to salve their consciences, and good money for any itch they have in their palms.'

'You don't have no 'igh opinion of folks,' the landlord answered him.

He didn't sleep well in the Clerkenwell tenement that night. Before dawn found him up and walking south to Field's printing works in Blackfriars.

'Careless of you,' was the printer's casual response when Palmer gave him a version of events. 'And the man you attacked outside the works when you were last here, he died you know.'

'He was after Government property, Mr Field.'

He wasn't, but that was the best story to give. The dead man's purple face and staring eyes came back into Palmer's mind. It had not yet entered his dreams. He had no feeling in the matter. What was evident was that Field wasn't going to help, Palmer decided as he walked away from the printworks. On the other hand, he wasn't likely to help the fugitive either, not now.

Enquiries on Bankside drew no sightings. Palmer headed for the actors' alehouse. Phillips was there, engaged in some company housekeeping business, but no Hemmings.

'I missed our friend in Stratford,' Palmer lied as dryly as he could.

Phillips looked up but said nothing.

'He was headed back here to London,' Palmer said.

'I'm due up in front of the Privy Council on Wednesday,' Phillips told him, leaving Palmer in no doubt who he blamed.

'Sorry about that. Just tell them the truth, it's all they want to hear. You're an actor, you've appeared in front of the like before.'

'Under better circumstances.'

'If our friend contacts you, tell him to turn himself into me – a message at the Bell in Carter Lane will find me.'

'Surely,' Phillips said but plainly did not mean.

'If he does, it'll go better with him – and you – and I can do something to protect his family. Do you have a family, Mr Phillips?'

The actor looked up angrily.

'Are you threatening my family?'

'No, just asking you to use your imagination from your friend Shakespeare's point of view. But before I go, there's one thing you *can* do for me.'

Palmer asked where Shakespeare deposited his money.

'Perhaps you want to put me to the trouble of obtaining legal authority?' he bluffed.

Phillips squirmed.

'No, no ... it's the same man the company uses.'

Palmer drew little co-operation from the goldsmith named.

'I'll need a magistrate's order to look into his deposits,' the man insisted.

'So he *has* money deposited with you,' Palmer said. 'It would be unwise of you to release any of it to him, legal order or no.'

The goldsmith appeared to take the hint.

It is now a matter of time, Palmer told himself, time he didn't have. If he came up with nothing what was he going to tell Cecil, and when?

On instinct he went to nearby St Paul's Churchyard. The centre of the book trade, it might be the last place Shakespeare could be expected to be found, but still ...

He passed the bookstall where he'd frightened the life out of its owner over the Richard play. The bookseller was there. He turned away as soon as he saw Palmer.

Palmer was hungry. He hasn't eaten since Stratford, he reminded himself, over two days ago. Thank God for beer! He went in search of Alice's pie stall.

'Funny that,' she greeted him, 'two in one day!'

Palmer was surprised.

'You and whatsisname, two in one day!'

Palmer's jaw froze in the act of biting.

'Shakespeare?'

'He can shake what 'e likes. Who else did you think I meant?'

'When was this?' he asked, containing his excitement.

'This morning. Not 'ere, up near Silver Street, you know, where I live.'

'I thought you said he lived on Bankside.'

'I thought so too,' Alice admitted, 'but I did see 'im right enough, coming out of the Mountjoys. Their house, it's in Silver Street. They takes in lodgers. They're *French*, they makes costume stuff for the playhouses.'

Silver Street in Cripplegate ward, just inside the walls near where Palmer lived – a Huguenot district. It was a clever place to go to ground, Palmer reckoned, close to a tiny exit gate from the City. The authorities left the locals to run their own affairs.

He gave Alice a generous silver groat.

'*You* can come again,' she called out after him.

On Silver Street he surveyed the house on the corner from the other side of the road. It was three storeys high with its shop on the ground floor. Its tenants he had already checked with a verger in the church behind him – the Mountjoys, the man had confirmed to him.

He spent an hour watching for sign of his quarry but without any luck. He was running out of time. He decided that he had to go in.

Two women, mother and daughter he assumed by their looks, were the barrier.

'I've come to see Mr Shakespeare,' he said quietly.

'We 'ave no-one of that name 'ere,' the older woman replied.

'*Madame est très gentille.*'

Madame fluttered and smiled.

'*Merci bien monsieur, mais comme vous parlez bien le français, monsieur!*'

'*Ce n'est pas vrai, madame.*'

'Shall I say to Mr Shakespeare he has a visitor, mother?'

Madame bridled at her daughter's indiscretion but the cat was out of the bag. She reapplied her smile in the direction of the visitor.

'Your name, monsieur?'

Palmer had already looked beyond the two women into the staircase behind. It was the only way out from the floors above as far as he could judge. All the same, he wasn't taking any chances. People jumped from windows if they had no other choice.

'*Un vieil ami,*' he said, striding past them and their protests.

He found his man in a small room under the sloping roof. A glance to the window was quickly suppressed. Shakespeare raised his hands in mock surrender.

'How did you find me here?'

Palmer never revealed his sources. He had informers everywhere was the impression he liked to create. Shakespeare understood.

'The Mountjoys know nothing about the trouble I'm in,' he said. 'As far as they're concerned, they're helping me while I find proper lodgings. They're in the theatre business.'

'I believe you,' Palmer said, 'I have no quarrel with them.'

'But you do with me. What can I say? The chance presented itself. I went, like any other captured animal would.'

'So, who was your accomplice?'

Shakespeare looked at his questioner with surprise then laughed in his high swooping sound.

'I have no idea, no, really, none! It was the last thing in the world I was expecting, but, there it was, the cage opened and I flew out.'

'You ask me to believe that?'

'How did you find me?' he asked again.

'It's my job.'

'What are you going to do now?'

Palmer began to unbutton his doublet.

'Something I should have done a while back...'

He took out Cecil's warrant from inside his doublet, settling himself on a stool.

'I'm going to question you formally.'

There was a pen and inkpot on what served as a desk in the room. Palmer borrowed it for his own business. He turned the warrant over.

'The nature of your relationship with Henry Wriothesley, Lord Southampton?'

Shakespeare looked at him askance. Palmer waved his pen to get an answer.

'Patron and poet,' the man said at last.

'Nothing more?'

'In so far as his position and mine allowed, friendship.'

'Friendship,' Palmer wrote down. 'Close friendship?'

'Not so, given our respective positions.'

'The friendship of an older for a younger man?'

'If you mean an older man wanting well for the younger – to marry and have children.'

'Impartial friendship then, for this lovely boy … more lovely and more temperate than a summer's day … beauty's pattern, lord of my love, my better angel – I'm quoting from your own writings. Shall I go on?'

'You know the answer to that, it's in the same sonnet.'

'Nature pricking him out for women's pleasure? Yes, well, why not? An unusual friendship just the same, between an actor and a nobleman, or a poet and his patron, wouldn't you agree?'

'It wouldn't be the first.'

Palmer stopped writing. He looked up as he asked the next question.

'The sonnets are *love* poetry.'

'Oh Mr Palmer, a poet needs inspiration and matter to work with, surely you understand that?'

'And poets write in this explicit style to men?'

'They write in … admiration.'

'In *ad-mir-ation*,' Palmer repeated as he wrote it down.

Shakespeare shrugged.

A question ran through Palmer's head, not for the first time.

Was there any physical expression of this 'love' between them? Sex, Mr Shakespeare – did sex take place between you? Would Cecil want to know? He might – such smears of unnatural practice had their uses – and he might not. Both suspects were married men, and yet, Southampton, he'd had a juicy reputation in his time with both sexes, or so Palmer had heard. And as for actors, they fucked anything that moved – or so the word was, omnifutuant, excellent word. Well, it wasn't a matter for him, Palmer decided, not when he had something firmer to pursue, something more incriminating.

'The Bassano affair – she was less important to you than him. What is it you write to him? Ah yes –that she has *thee* is of my wailing chief.'

'Who would you sacrifice first, Mr Palmer, your paying patron, the one keeping you alive while disease runs wild and your place of work is closed, or your bedmate of the moment?'

'And that's what she was?'

'I'm a man, away from home for most of the year. She wasn't the first.'

'And these *others* have sonnets in their name as well?'

Shakespeare laughed, more discretely this time.

'You can find them here and there in my plays.'

… in variant forms of the one dark woman, he did not say.

Palmer gathered himself for a fresh attack.

'The sonnets appear to put an end to things, yet there was continuing contact between you and Southampton, as recently as last year at the playhouse, according to your colleagues.'

'Plays are popular events, Mr Palmer, thousands come to see them.'

'So I am told. Did he come with his smart friends, say what? I helped make Master Shakespeare what he is? Did he earn the right to one very special favour?'

'The Richard play? You are obsessed by it!'

'The Queen is, Mr Shakespeare, she talks of little else which is why we're here. What I cannot fathom is why you did it, with everything there was at stake, for yourself, for your colleagues at the Globe, for your family?'

The last word triggered something else in Palmer's head, something he never liked to think about. Why had his father done it? Ruined the Palmer family? The angry question would not let go, running in and out of the business at hand in the investigator's mind. Why? Not only held to the old faith but actively proselytised it, shouted it from the pulpit and in the street to the destruction of his family and himself? What moved these madmen to act in such a way?

'The hold Southampton had over you must have been so *strong*,' Palmer said, trying to blot out the other voice. Just like your father and his faith, the voice insisted. 'Oh, he'd have been sharp enough to get his people to talk to yours to avoid suspicion, to Phillips and Hemmings, fools attracted by the glitter of cheap money.' His father, now, he could just have paid the fines and worshipped in the old way in private, but no...

No answer came to either question.

'When the game was up you ran.' His father hadn't run. He had stood proud. They took him down all the same.

'Everything you say is surmise, without any proof,' he heard his prisoner say. It was a darned sight cannier than the imprecations of hellfire his father had hurled at his persecutors.

'Proof! Proof is a very cheap commodity in times like these, easily bought and sold,' he fired back – as faith had been for his father, and for all the generations of Palmers he'd nonetheless reduced to nothing, his son included.

'Is it? Is it to you?' Shakespeare leaned forward. 'Assume that you're right. Why does that lead me to commit treason? I have, as you say, a lot to lose. I made my choice years ago – not Southampton but the drama, not the private house of the wealthy but the public stage of the penny payer. I'm a man of my own means now. Why would I throw that up?'

'Because *he* asked you to.' As God had asked his own father?

It would not be what the Chief Minister wanted to hear.

~ 14 ~

I<small>T WAS TIME</small> to take Shakespeare into Whitehall and Robert Cecil, Palmer decided. He had the man, he had sufficient evidence for further questions to be asked by the authorities and answered.

He led Shakespeare through the door of the penthouse room. Halfway down the stairs, they were met by what looked like the man of the house. At his back were a couple of apprentices, bent on looking handy, clutching staves. Not much use in the confined space all the same, Palmer reckoned, his right hand clenching involuntarily, his left making ready to reach the dagger in his boot. He was not going to be cheated, not this time. He would do whatever was needed.

Each side waited for the other to make a move.

'It's all right, my friends,' Shakespeare said, 'I am just going out to help this gentleman with some playhouse business.'

The apprentices looked to their master. The man of the house was not convinced.

'Will you be coming back?' he asked suspiciously.

'Yes, of course. Please, let us by.'

The men gave way.

Palmer breathed a sigh of relief – to have lost his prisoner twice would have been careless. There was a second stab of relief, that he had not been called to action. He knew just what he was capable of. Was there something of his father in that, twisted into a different pattern? He wasted no time in getting himself and his prisoner out of the building.

'We're going to walk.'

'Where to?' the prisoner asked.

'To Whitehall.'

The afternoon light was beginning to close in by the time the pair arrived. While they waited to be seen, Palmer gathered news from the chief official.

The trial of Essex and Southampton was the day after tomorrow, in Westminster Hall nearby. The peers chosen to make up the jury had already been notified. Some of those named bore old grudges against the two accused.

'What are the charges?' Palmer asked.

'Lord Essex is accused of attempting to usurp the crown.'

Bad news for the author of a play about usurpation.

'The accusation against Lord Southampton is one of conspiring to depose and kill the Queen and overturn the government.'

Palmer whistled. The stakes were high.

'Several of the leading insurgents have already made helpful confessions.'

Palmer bet they had, and entirely freely!

'Any of the top men?' he cross-quizzed the official.

'One has decided to turn Queen's evidence. The prosecuting counsel have also been appointed.'

'Oh, yes?'

'The main prosecutor is Attorney-General Coke assisted by Francis Bacon.'

Fiery Coke and slippery Bacon- always on the right side at the right time. The two men were known to hate one other, now they were a pair of hounds vying with each other to be in at the kill.

'Wasn't Bacon...'

'Close to Lord Essex? Yes indeed, and doubly valuable because he can expose the private ambitions of the accused.'

The cards were well and truly stacked.

At last Palmer was summoned. He left his prisoner under guard in the antechamber.

The Chief Minister looked up only when the investigator was standing in front of him.

'You have him?' Cecil asked. 'Good, your report then.'

Palmer was brief. He confirmed his finding that there was a continuing connection between Southampton and Shakespeare, connection giving grounds for suspicion of collusion. There was nothing said about the incident on the road to London or the fugitive's flight. Never tell the client what he didn't need to know...

'Why would he do that?' Cecil asked, seeing the problems these findings would give him in advocating pardon for Southampton.

'It's here in these.'

Palmer pushed the thick sheaf of sonnets across the table.

'You gave me a dozen, I found a dozen times as many. There's a seam running through them, the bond of Shakespeare to Southampton. They explain everything.'

'Our man admits it?'

'He denies it.'

Cecil riffled unenthusiastically through the pile of papers in front of him.

'Leaving aside private passions, is it your opinion that it was Southampton who was responsible for the Richard play? If so, does this of necessity prove treasonable intent?'

'You asked me to investigate the nature of the connection between the two suspects. I've shown that it's much deeper and long-lasting than was at first thought.'

Why couldn't he be like everyone else and just deliver what was expected? God damn the stubborn Palmer character!

'Well then, let's call him in.'

A nod to the chief official was quickly obeyed.

Shakespeare came in. To Palmer's astonishment, Cecil offered him his hand.

'Welcome, welcome. Let me say, before we begin, that I have admired and enjoyed your work on many occasions. My question is a simple one. Before I ask it, please allow me a few words.'

Cecil walked to the far side of the room as if he were rehearsing what he had to say. He turned back to face them.

'Men sometimes do strange things. Ten days ago Lords Essex and Southampton rode out at the head of a band of armed men, many of them experienced soldiers. If they had turned left to Whitehall, who could have stopped them? The Queen would have been their prisoner. Do you believe that she would have agreed to dismiss her Government? No, nor do I.'

He smiled as he said it, as if sharing the joke.

'So the insurgents must have been prepared to do their worst.'

Cecil looked keenly at Shakespeare. Nothing came back. He took the next step.

'For some reason they appealed to the City – to the mob as well as to the money, a mob intended to have been aroused by a suggestive drama.'

Palmer was watching Shakespeare. The man was still giving nothing away.

'What surprises me is this, and it comes back to the question of acting in or out of character – I have seen your plays, so when I ask myself, does their author think that *this* is the way to manage the nation's affairs, I cannot believe you think that it is. It may be the way of Lord Essex, but is it yours? To put armed villains on the streets, to attempt to inflame the people for narrow reasons of self- interest or wounded feelings? God knows, we live in difficult times, but where is the sense in staging selfish acts of rebellion, where is the policy in that? Now Mr Palmer here would have me believe that your better sense was overcome by private loyalties.'

Cecil let the question hang in the air, inviting response.

Shakespeare took his time to answer.

'Mr Palmer ... Mr Palmer relies on documents which are many years old and come from another time. Of actual evidence, he offers nothing. He is a master of circumstance.'

Cecil held his hand up when Palmer tried to answer. The politician spoke again, this time in a harsher voice.

'Did Lord Southampton, in any way, directly or indirectly, through you or not, put your company up to perform the play in question and with seditious intent? Please think as a fellow subject of our Queen, not as one man's friend.'

'No, I do not believe so.'

'Can you be sure so?'

'He did not, as far as I know, do what you suggest.'

'But he could have, without your knowledge?'

Shakespeare refused the escape ladder offered him.

'I do not believe that he did.'

Cecil played with the papers in front of him.

'I have reason to believe that Lord Southampton's defence will be that he was mixed up in the affair out of misguided loyalty to his friend and mentor, Lord Essex. If so, he might say that those who commissioned the play acted on their own initiative. He might distance himself.'

Finger the little men, Palmer took him to mean, doing what they thought the big men wanted.

'Mr Bacon is a clever man, subtle – have you met him? Yes? An extremely able advocate, too. I also understand that he might, if the play comes up in the trial, take an interesting line.'

Palmer smelled a ploy. Bacon had gone over from Essex to the Government. His job was to nail Essex down to the charge. Surely Shakespeare was never going to be allowed to be the substitute for the main target. Southampton was another matter.

'Mr Bacon's approach, oh, it might avoid accusing Lord Southampton of being the instigator, in the matter of the play that is. You see, Mr Bacon might say that the idea did *not* come from Lord Southampton at all. He might say that the idea came from *you*, Mr Shakespeare.'

Palmer was amazed. So, by his look, was Shakespeare.

'Oh, I don't think so either, Mr Shakespeare, but you see, our problem is that Mr Bacon might say it. He has a duty to the court to explore every byway in the case. The question is – do you think Lord Southampton will *deny* it, deny that the fault was yours? With all that is at stake?'

Perfect, Palmer judged, just perfect. If Shakespeare could rely on his friend to answer truthfully – that whoever's the idea was, it wasn't Shakespeare's – then there wasn't an ounce of risk, not to the actor or to everything he had achieved – the money, the big house, the coat of arms and the genteel future for his family line.

But if the poet believed that Southampton would grab at any lifeline thrown to him ... Palmer sucked his teeth – it was a big throw of the dice for the actor to make.

Shakespeare's words came out slowly.

'So ... I suggested the play ... to Lord Southampton?'

'More than that – Mr Bacon is too clever by half sometimes. No, Mr Bacon might be minded to suggest, not only that it *was* you who suggested it ...'

Re-minded, Palmer guessed. The prosecutors wouldn't make a single move, not one, without rehearsing it with the powers-that-be and that meant Cecil himself.

'... only, not to him, no, you suggested it to someone else, one of the *minor* players in the affair, doing your bit to help the cause.'

The idea of the Richard play was to be Shakespeare's; even better, Southampton knew nothing about it. Palmer's eyes shifted to Shakespeare. Would he be prepared to sacrifice himself for the younger man this time? Would he play the noble part he had so often written in his plays, or scramble for safety like everyone else within the shabby reality of life?

'What do you want from me?' Shakespeare asked.

'The answer to my original question,' Cecil said.

Shakespeare paused on the edge of the moment. Finally he spoke.

'The Richard play was not my suggestion.'

He had something more to say.

'It wasn't my suggestion, but I couldn't oppose him.'

'So you knew,' Cecil said.

Shakespeare looked away. He tried to speak, stopped, then spoke again.

'I pretended to myself not to know.'

'I'm surprised he cracked,' Palmer said to Cecil once they were left alone.

'I am not,' said Cecil. 'I gave him no choice, because it's only blind chance which has put him in the opposite camp. Deep down, he knows that reason stands with us, not with

Essex and Southampton. But when head clashes with heart, there is always a price to pay.'

'Was it wise to trust him to go out on parole and return for the trial?'

Cecil waved his agent's concern aside.

'Now, about what we've just witnessed,' he said, lowering his voice to the level of confidentiality, 'tell no-one, write it down nowhere, not even for my people. This must remain entirely between us.'

He pushed across the table a large purse of money. It came with fresh instructions.

'Meet Shakespeare at the trial at the time we ordered and find a place where he can see and *be seen* by the defendants, especially by Southampton.'

Palmer picked up his purse and turned to leave.

'You've forgotten something,' Cecil said.

He pushed the packet of sonnets back across the table. What did that mean, Palmer asked himself as he picked the package up? Why ever would the Chief Minister want nothing like these papers on record?

~ 15 ~

A DAY PASSED.

One man spent it in near-silence in the company of his actor friends in the alehouse, near the playhouse still closed by Government decree.

The other lived it up in his favourite drinking hole on Government money.

In the Tower, two noble prisoners paced their cells, one practising his defence, the other berating God for denying him in his hour of need.

A woman turned restlessly in her bed, agonising about a trial she had no wish to go to.

It was the hour after dawn.

Palmer shivered as an icy wind blew down the river, huddling himself as low in the boat as he could in front of a silent waterman on the way to Whitehall stairs. Through gaps in the fog he could see evidence of troops lined up, guarding the watersides. What were they expecting? The answer was nothing and everything, whatever might be provoked by the two notorious prisoners about to be transported separately under heavy guard along the same river passage.

The Government was taking no chances, including the outlandish risk of a bid to free the accused men once they were away from the Tower. It said something about the state of the country to Palmer when the authorities feared a bunch of washed-up has-beens.

He disembarked at Whitehall stairs and waited at the appointed place. Another boat discharged its cargo, William Shakespeare. Cecil had been right about him being reliable.

Clocks struck the hour of nine around Whitehall.

From his place inside Westminster Hall, Palmer heard the crowd hush momentarily as they watched the main actors in the trial begin taking their places on the stage beneath the ancient hammerbeam roof. It was a solemn, ordered entry designed to create a spectacle of the highest political effect.

The Lord High Steward led the way to his presiding seat – once a poet and the author of plays before ambition pushed the writer's pen aside. In the man's swagger in his robes of authority Palmer measured his deliberate distance from his past. The two Lord Chief Justices flanked him – one of them with his own score to settle, for being locked up by the insurgents in Essex House during the violence of the Sunday before last. So much for unbiased judgement! A squad of judges, a kernel of scarlet among the regiment of functionaries was busily packing the rest of the bench. As they settled in, the noise in the watching crowd grew back to its earlier level.

Palmer counted twenty-five in the jury, all peers. One, he had heard, had only just been let out of prison for an assault on Southampton. So this was a man being given – and wholeheartedly taking – a second crack at his enemy through the machinery of the State – well, well.

His eye turned to the prosecution team, drawn by the brilliant Francis Bacon, once loyal to Essex, now his intending nemesis. A silent assassin sort, Palmer decided in contrast to the leading man type presented by his bigger, more handsome neighbour, Attorney-General Coke.

He felt a presence at this elbow. He turned to see Cecil's chief official.

'Splendid roof,' the man said, looking upwards, 'built by King Richard two hundred years ago.'

... the same Richard in the play which had caused so much fuss. Men and their trials may come and go, Palmer reflected yet, the roof stayed sound.

Security was tight. The judges were defended by a squad of sergeants-at-arms backed up by the Queen's Guard, including a company of Yeomen. Not a chance, the old soldier in Palmer calculated, if anyone fancied their chances of a courtroom rescue.

He caught sight of his old tutor Lambarde, no doubt here for the prospect of a juicy legal drama. They exchanged no marks of recognition, Lambarde was too clever for that, he understood.

Palmer saw no sign of the Globe actors – sensible men. Their colleague Shakespeare would have to do, he reckoned, checking on the man under his charge standing next to him. Shakespeare, he saw, was looking elsewhere. Palmer followed the line of his sight and found Emilia Lanier. Her eyes were fixed on the trial dais where the defendants were due to appear.

The crowd hushed again, straining forward. 'Essex, Southampton,' voices whispered in anticipation.

As if on cue, the two men strode onto the stage establishing the characters they wished their audience to believe. They embraced confidently. An atmosphere of silent curiosity pervaded the Hall, Palmer included. How would they behave – remorsefully or not? Rumours of how they had been taking their imprisonment and trial were conflicting. Here today, Essex looked cheerful, or was pretending to be, wearing his 'I have no case to answer' look. Southampton was dressed in a dark suit with a long-sleeved gown to hide agitated hands. The curl of the young man's lip had disappeared. How much hope had he left in him?

'How do you plead,' an official voice demanded after the heavy indictments were read.

'Not guilty!'

A low sound came from the crowd, meaning what? Surprise, or interest in the chance of a more argumentative trial hearing? Palmer looked to Essex who was over-miming an all-round show of mocking disbelief that such charges could ever have been brought – you must believe me, he appeared to be saying! Unwise, Palmer told himself, unwise. Southampton's plea was more respectful, directed towards those on the dais who held his life in their hands. Please believe me!

Attorney-General Coke, the star prosecutor stood up first for the prosecution. His voice roared from the floor and rang in the rafters. His vocal setting was single and loud.

'Anyone who raises his own forces in a time of settled Government, the Law is clear that it is *high* treason. If he acts to usurp the Government, the Law declares that he *must* intend the *death* of the monarch. And where he assembles his own forces and then, when his sovereign commands him to stand them down, he continues in this course of action, there can be *no question* that it is high treason!'

Coke cast an imperious look around him as if defying anyone to suggest otherwise. But he was only warming up. Now came his opportunity to blacken the characters of the defendants, damn their ingratitude to the Queen and let rip with a final fulmination directed at Essex.

'You were set on summoning a Parliament where you intended to preside in a *blood*-red robe!'

Red with the blood of the Queen, everyone understood, red as the robes of the judges of the realm who would have been replaced in a new order by a supreme judge – Essex, according to Coke.

It was too much for the defendant who sprang to his feet.

'The Attorney-General is making speeches and they are *slanders*, pleading innocent men out of their lives.'

Coke's snarl shifted to a smile. He had achieved what he wanted, Palmer could see, got under Essex's skin.

The court now called for evidence which followed in a welter of statements. Some were patently concocted by offenders anxious to make deals.

Then the Chief Justice, the one who had suffered detention by the insurgents rose from the bench. He stepped down onto the floor of the court with a heavy tread. Venting his outrage at his treatment – judge and witness in one with popping eyes in mottled face like a put-upon rooster – he came too close to comedy for Palmer. The investigator stifled his laughter – contempt of this court would be an unwise risk to take. He cast a sly glance at Shakespeare next to him. The man's face betrayed nothing.

Essex protested.

'I did it for your own safety!'

The look of pure black spite from the judge nearly made Palmer laugh again. He noticed that Emilia Lanier appeared uncommitted in contrast to the many in the crowd clucking sympathy with the furious judge.

The commander of the Queen's Guard strutted forward to give evidence. Raleigh was known to hate Essex, for being younger, for supplanting him in the affections of his Queen, for the very sight and sound of him! He had had a secret meeting, he announced, with someone from the Essex camp on the morning of the insurrection.

'He told me we would have a bloody day of it.'

A murmur ran round the Hall. So the uprising was expected, it was not spur-of-the-moment. Wasn't that what Raleigh was saying?

His witness was called. Palmer did not like the look of him – the man reeked of double-agency. Neither did Essex, who went onto the attack against him.

'Did you ever advise me to hold back?'

'I think I did,' came the witness's lame reply.

'It is not the time to be talking about thinking. Some things ought not to be forgotten.'

It was a victory for Essex, but a small one against the overwhelming odds of the State apparatus ranged around the Hall against him.

The witness statements which followed were all remarkably concordant.

'Such miracles of consistency must surely attest to their truth.' Coke said it without the slightest hint of irony. He was the most dangerous type of lawyer to Palmer's mind, one without humour.

'Some interrogators can bring the most conflicting accounts together,' Essex protested, looking round for support. There was none on offer.

A hush of expectation greeted a change in prosecutor. Francis Bacon stepped forward almost without anyone noticing. Palmer looked again towards Shakespeare at his side. The dramatist in him should force him to look up – this was the pivotal scene. He saw no reaction.

Nor did he see any reticence in Bacon's manner towards his former friend and patron. It was as if he and Essex had never met, or like a smaller actor stepping out of the shadow of a greater one, knowing that this performance could at last raise him up and cast the other down.

Bacon started in a low key, quietly and civilly.

'Tell me,' he asked with the voice of the reasonable man confronted with the unreasonable, 'the imprisonment of the Government spokesmen at Essex House, how was that justified?'

Essex appeared to lose every last shred of his temper. He broke into a tirade about something entirely different, challenging his examiner to get down to the real matter at stake. This was, Essex announced, the absence of a plan for the succession to the throne. The crowd responded – it was illegal even to mention it, Palmer knew. Essex was riding dangerously if he was about to carry the attack to the Chief Minister. It was like a champion from the days of old stepping forward to challenge an oppressive power.

'He said, my Lords, Secretary Cecil said that the Infanta of Spain's claim to the English throne, the Spanish claim my Lords, he said that it was as good as any other's! A member of the Privy Council told me,' Essex insisted, rolling his eyes in horror.

The implication was not lost on the Hall. Spain was hell to England's heaven, creator of an Armada launched to crush the nation back down under the superstitious rule of Rome. Essex had made his career fighting them. What kind of devious politics was Cecil being accused of? Where was he anyway, Palmer was not alone in thinking?

'I demand the name of this Privy Councillor!'

The voice belonged to Cecil. Where he had sprung from, Palmer had no idea.

A tiny, fragile figure now visible in the middle of the Hall, Cecil turned on Essex.

'I concede your superiority to me in rank and in fighting ability, but at least I stand here an innocent man whereas *you*, you are no better than a delinquent! God knows, I always supported you, and recommended you to Her Highness, as I would do now if … if I had not witnessed you attempt the *throne* itself!'

A buzz ran round the Hall. Cecil was playing for high stakes, dealing this card of high treason. The noble jurymen listened with closer attention – hearing the arch-diplomat Cecil angry was a rare experience.

Encouraged, the tiny figure was turning up the pressure on Essex, well known to have been brought up in the Cecil household. Essex was handsome, privileged by title, everything on the face of it which this son of the Cecil house was not and never could be. Was it a day of reckoning long in the making between them?

'If it were just a case of you alone then it would not be so bad but you have drawn others into your net, which I wish to *God* had never happened!'

Essex appeared dumbstruck, staggered by the heat of Cecil's outburst against him. It was as if he was hearing for the first time the reality of his own mistakes. He put up an ineffectual sneer, turning his back on his accuser.

Palmer was not alone in understanding one thing more – that Cecil was beginning to show his hand to the jury, about Southampton and others drawn by Essex into his net, those he 'wished to God' had not been. Would the jurors take the hint and make a separation in their minds between Essex and Southampton?

Cecil took a step forward, towards the shoulder turned coldly away from him.

'Name your informant if you dare!'

Essex turned round, this time only too happy to take him on.

'It's no invention, I promise you. Lord Southampton heard it as well as I did.'

Essex looked confidently towards his co-accused. Southampton shuffled awkwardly for all to see. Distance from Essex was his only hope for survival, everyone knew.

Cecil turned towards him too – the one man who was trying to help Southampton was now asking for his help. Muffled words from Southampton went unheard by many, but not by Palmer.

'He's asking the court if it's in order for him to give the name,' he whispered to Shakespeare.

Permission was given.

'I name...'

It was Essex's uncle, also one of the Government spokesmen locked up by Essex in the uprising. Which way would he testify? The noise in the Hall debated it.

Palmer did not envy the veteran court official who walked steadily into the court. He had the look on his face that he would rather be anywhere else than here. He appeared visibly torn between family and duty. Family was probably why he had made himself scarce that day, hoping to avoid testifying. Duty had seen him grow old and comfortable in the Queen's service.

He stood up in front of the court, patiently waiting for the inevitable question. Yes, he said, the Chief Minister had said something of the sort about the soundness of the Infanta's claim, but he had spoken in the context of a pamphlet which had been worrying him, propaganda backing the Spanish claim.

'What the Chief Minister said was this – it was *impertinent* of the writer to give the Infanta of Spain as much right as any of the other claimants.'

He bowed his head as he said it, aware of the consequences. He had blown to pieces Essex's wild theory about Cecil conspiring with the Spaniards. His evidence denied it.

Cecil went in for the kill.

'Your malice towards me,' he said to Essex, voice rising, 'flows from nothing more than *my* desire for peace' – with Spain, Palmer took him to mean – 'and yours for *war!*'

The whole Hall looked towards Essex. The man looked crushed. He opened his mouth as if to speak. Nothing came out. He retired to his seat, chin on hand to contemplate his position. What move was left open to him now?

It was Southampton's turn to face examination.

His case began no better than Essex's. Testimony from a friend that he had for years been unhappy at the Queen over his lack of prospects was topped by one final, terrible accusation read out by a prosecutor.

'It was my Lord Southampton who provoked Lord Essex into insurgency.'

The accusation audibly disturbed the court.

'With friends like that...' Palmer began to whisper to his charge.

The trial moved on. Afternoon succeeded morning.

Essex's final speech was not heard sympathetically, not in Palmer's opinion. It left his auditors apathetic, as if they judged it pointless and a waste of their time. His day, this play, their unspoken verdict seemed to say, was over a long time since. The actor was flagging in front of a lukewarm audience. It was time for his scene to close, was their will.

Southampton's case interested them more – he had, they judged, a sporting chance of survival. To Palmer's mind it would all depend on the line the young man took. Arrogance had already been tried that day by Essex without success.

'As to my part in the rebellion and the claims made today that it was actuated by discontent against the Crown, *I deny it!*'

Southampton looked around him, paused for effect, lowered his voice.

'The truth is, I acted out of *loyalty* – to my kinsman and my friend the Earl of Essex.'

In that one sentence he was shifting the burden of responsibility, everyone understood. It was all Essex's fault.

Essex showed no reaction. Didn't he realise what was happening or was he too exhausted?

Southampton's voice began to grow in confidence as Essex's energy ebbed.

'As to what we planned to do, I cannot deny it, but those plans were not carried out. I accompanied my friend to the City to defend him against his *private* enemies. I did not hear the Government order to disassemble or I would have obeyed it. When we came back to Essex House I did everything in my power to prevent physical resistance.'

That's a lie, Palmer knew first hand.

Southampton fixed his eyes on the judges and then the jury.

'From what I am admitting now, I submit that no evidence of treason can be drawn. Therefore I beg the court *not* to judge me by the strict letter of the law but as you may be convinced, by me, that I *intended*.'

Ah, the issue of intent at last, Palmer told himself, clever. He glanced over to Lambarde in the crowd of onlookers. He was smiling too – so the young Earl's brief exposure to the law had not been entirely wasted. Southampton had rung all the changes, from not knowing to not doing to having no intention, with a plea in mitigation thrown in at the end for his conduct in preventing excessive bloodshed! He was giving the court plenty of rope to spare him.

Foxy, Palmer decided as he watched the Earl, his colour back up and a calculating look about the green-grey eyes, but lying just the same.

Was it now for the first time that Southampton caught sight of Shakespeare? A boyish smile radiated across the young man's face. Then it faded, like a mirror catching a reflected message, one of warning. Beware the crowd, it seemed to say, it can turn on you.

Palmer looked over to where Emilia Lanier was. She was still in her place, her face entirely convinced by the actor onstage in front of them all.

The jury took no more than an hour to deliver its verdicts – both men guilty as charged. The crowd let out a collective, satisfied grunt.

Southampton played his final card.

'I do not despair of the Queen's mercy.'

It had no effect on the Lord High Steward. He had promotion in view, Palmer had heard from Cecil's chief official, if he did what was necessary.

'You shall both be taken from your place of imprisonment to the place of your execution, there to be hanged by the neck and taken down alive, and your bowels taken out and your heart burned in front of your eyes, your bodies to be quartered – and so may God have mercy on your souls.'

It was the most horrible form of execution available – the guilty men, born among the highest in the land were to be treated as common criminals. A second grunt of satisfaction ran through the crowd, looking forward to the holiday entertainment it promised.

The crowd was quick to disperse, carrying Palmer and Shakespeare along with it. It ran them up against Emilia Lanier. Holding her arm, about to steer her away from any public expression of grief was a man Palmer assumed to be the husband. He was large and pink of face.

Palmer was almost past them when something remembered stopped him in his tracks. He turned to take a second look. He had seen that face before. It wasn't a good memory. Was it a face in a dream? Something like that, moving away from him, out of his reach – the figure on the road back from Stratford!

It fell into place – Emilia's husband. But why?

Palmer walked straight back, stiff with anger. Lanier was babbling to Shakespeare, deliberately keeping his back to Palmer, shutting him out.

'Weren't you close to Southampton, wasn't he your patron in the old days?' Palmer heard him saying. 'I fought with both of them against the Spaniards. It's a perilous world, my masters.'

Palmer planted himself in front of him. Lanier avoided Palmer's stare. He persisted with Shakespeare.

'You know my wife Emilia?'

Had he no idea of the past between him and her? Palmer saw a wary smile flicker around the actor's mouth.

'This is a day we can't forget,' Emilia said, plucking at the fragile web of the past, prompting Lanier to act before she tore it down.

'You must pardon us.'

Let him go, for the time being, Palmer promised himself, watching Lanier bustle his wife away through the throng.

PALMER WENT with Shakespeare to see him off downriver from Whitehall stairs. As they waited for a boat, Palmer spoke quietly to him.

'The sentence isn't yet confirmed, it's up to the Queen.'

'A terrible death,' Shakespeare said, looking out across the river at the fog rolling in.

Palmer spared the actor what he really thought, that it was no more than Southampton deserved. He was a man betrayed by his own character, spending years causing trouble until, in the end, he set Essex up and sent him to the gibbet; a selfish child of mischief, conscious of little but himself.

A boat came. Shakespeare got into it without looking back.

He was not the only passenger known to Palmer embarking on the river at this time. The Laniers were still on the north bank, enlarged to a group of four. The extra two were a woman and a child – Emilia's boy and the maidservant, Palmer recognised them to be.

It was a strange time to bring a lad to Westminster to see its sights on such a day. Was it to remind him of the world his mother believed he belonged to, this byblow of nobility?

Only, the lad bore no resemblance to Southampton or to the Hunsdon strain as far as Palmer could see. He watched Emilia running her hand through his unruly shock of hair, a maternal act which Palmer was about to ignore until another memory stopped him in his tracks. Where had he seen hair that colour before? Not here in London. He racked his brain. It was ... a girl's hair ... Shakespeare's girl! It was Susanna's hair, its auburn colour, same as her father's – what he had left of it; same as this boy's.

Well, well, what a surprise – Emilia's bastard boy, neither Hunsdon's nor Southampton's, more likely fathered by no better than a base player! O Emilia, what a joke! True, the father was a man who had no heir male to inherit his hard-won coat of arms. Well, here the heir was, staring him in the face with a bastard bend sinister to match.

Not that any of them would want to hear it, let alone admit it, such was their stubborn way. Not by *him*, he could hear Emilia say; not by *her*, the player's vehement reply. Only the boy might be made happier by the knowledge ... but since when did a child's wishes come into it?

Palmer debated what to do with his finding. A morsel for the ear of the Chief Minister. Or for his chief official, to put in one of his notes on the file?

No, he decided, it was too small for Cecil and not nearly gross enough for what Lanier deserved, the man on the road. Palmer felt his right fist clenching.

'Mr Palmer?'

The interruption came from Cecil's chief official. The agent was wanted by the Chief Minister.

Palmer was made to wait for some hours all the same on account of heavy business in the aftermath of the trial.

'A satisfactory end to a difficult day,' Cecil said when they finally met, back to his normal, calmer self.

'Was it?'

Cecil shot Palmer a curious look.

'From the point of view of the Essex business, I'm bound to say that it was. As far as Southampton goes...'

He spread his hands in uncertainty.

'He *was* helpful, over the Spanish business,' Palmer suggested.

'Yes, he was. I have already received the usual pleading letters about him from – let me see – his wife, his mother – oh – and from his brother-in-law, only *he* does not want him saved at all but would like us to give him his property now that Southampton is about to give up his earthly state! One is spared nothing of human nature in my position.'

'So what will you do, sir?'

Cecil thought for a moment.

'I will continue to try to save him, and I might just succeed if the Queen will get over the Richard play and allow herself to believe that it is *unwise* to cut off too many heads in present times. It only makes the rest of us nervous. On our side is the fact that she doesn't like signing death warrants, but I would not want to rely on that alone.'

In case she applied the same indecision to Essex?

'What else can be done?' Palmer asked.

'Good question. Perhaps,' Cecil began to say, walking up and down in thought, 'perhaps if Essex would publicly admit just how *far* he was prepared to go, how ruthlessly he had intended to act, it would help us with the doubters. We could grant him a private execution, the blade rather than the rope and all the rest of that bloody business. He is a man for whom appearances are important. If we had Essex's confession, then he will be the tethered scapegoat and Southampton can live, rotting in the Tower at Her Highness's pleasure.'

'How would Essex be persuaded?'

'He dies like a gentleman and we go easy on his family – his son and heir in particular – once he's out of the way for good.'

'He'll never agree to it.'

'No, fools always resist the best solution.'

Yes, Palmer thought, about his own father and why he was standing where he was today, doing what he was doing.

Cecil stopped his pacing.

'But *that* is where Southampton comes in. He wants to live, so we must get him to agree that they all wanted the Queen dead. He tells Essex that we know it, Essex confesses and goes out in style – admission of treason, a pretty speech at the scaffold and then, off with his head!'

'And Shakespeare? Are we finished with him?'

'He has a powerful protector in Lord Hunsdon. Hunsdon's busy going round saying that the Richard play is all a fuss about nothing. Perhaps the Queen will start to believe him. Nonetheless, I think that there's more to be gained from our author friend.'

'The Southampton connection?'

'Yes, we may have something there. Consider this – we need Southampton to persuade Essex to confess, in his interest and ours. It would be very like Southampton to turn me down out of what? I do not know, spite let us say, so ... let Shakespeare act as the *conduit* for the deal, Shakespeare to Southampton, Southampton to Essex, and the rest follows.'

'What do you want me to do?'

'Simple, you handle Shakespeare, watch him do it, *make* him do it if you have to.'

'And the benefit to him?'

'Do you have to ask? As matters stand, he's expendable on a par with some of the minnows around Essex who must also go the same way...'

Only not the same way, Palmer told himself, no swift fall of the blade but a dangle on the end of a rope followed by the carving out of their innards while their eyes could still see it and then a rotting of their quartered parts in public places for all to see and smell.

'So do what he is bid and he lives. He has already come a long way in life. He has too much to lose.'

Including the nice manor house in Stratford, Palmer reminded himself with a flicker of envy. The lost home in Kent was no bigger.

'Yes,' Cecil said, 'he saves Southampton too, the man you reckon was his muse.'

'What do you suggest?' Palmer asked.

'A small and a larger gesture. There will be a crowd of witnesses when Essex exits our world precisely because we do not want any legends cropping up – he never really died, he's awaiting the call, that sort of thing. The witnesses will be gentlemen, to see fair play and to remind them of their own duty. I understand that Mr Shakespeare *is* a gentleman, coat of arms and all. We should value a keener sense of judgement from him in future.'

'Can you be sure you'll get it?'

'I have always taken him to be one of our less strident authors. On top of that, we have marked his cards and we have our ways of making life difficult for him – the censor can turn witchhunter if we order him to, lucrative bookings for his company at court and from the nobility would dry up, if we hint as much. He would soon be disowned by his fellows, his earnings would dwindle from a stream to a trickle ... yet I would prefer a different outcome.'

And what might that be, Palmer wanted to ask but knew it was not his place to.

'I want,' Cecil said, giving equal emphasis to both words, 'to attract him to our side, once Essex is despatched and Southampton is safely locked away. It is as well to tune the playhouses as well as the pulpits in these times of change.'

'You mentioned a larger gesture,' Palmer reminded him, more concerned about his own instructions rather than policies of State.

Cecil's voice turned grave.

'The execution of the Earl of Essex will be no easy matter for the Queen, whatever people may think. He was her favourite, her last reminder of her youth. She overlooked his rashness several times before we in Government were able to persuade her to take a harder line towards him.'

Getting her to sign the death warrant was going to take time, Palmer knew as well as did the man in front of him, involving every trick in the book, of her evasion and their persuasion.

'She is a woman, she will be distraught at his loss, he is the last flower of summer to her autumn eye. As a consequence I have had a word with the Master of the Revels and his superior, Lord Hunsdon. We are planning as many distractions for her as we can. The day before the execution, we shall have a play at court. It would be extremely *wise* for Mr Shakespeare's company to accept the invitation to perform – not that Tilney or Hunsdon will give them any choice! Tragedy should be avoided, comedy might be tactless … a romance could go well … but these are details. To answer your question, you are to stick to our man like a limpet during the days ahead to see that he does whatever we ask of him.'

'So my immediate orders are?'

'Get Shakespeare to put the deal to Southampton. The rest follows.'

Where Palmer found Lanier later that night was a rough alehouse not so far but far away enough from his house in St James's, one where the barmaids were versatile. He made sure that Lanier did not see him. The man was too busy groping a girl to notice.

He waited for him outside, near the entrance of a small, crooked alleyway. Soon Lanier came by, drunk and spent.

He could have had no idea what hit him.

Palmer started with a crippling knee to the man's groin then banged his face hard against a wall. Among the smell of shit and piss in the alleyway, Lanier retched violently. Palmer yanked his head back a second time, slammed it forcibly against the wall and pressed it hard against the brickwork. Blood was running down Lanier's chin and onto the wall in a darkly shining stain.

'I have no money,' he gasped.

Palmer forced Lanier's arm up his back to breaking point.

'I have, plenty, enough to buy a new hat ... the old one got a bullet through it ... on the road from Stratford.'

Palmer felt Lanier's body slump in resignation. He wheeled the bigger man round.

'Oh my God – Palmer!'

'Now, tell me the whole story.'

Palmer tightened his grip.

'My wife, Emilia ... said you had to be stopped ... you were going to turn me in ... as one of the rebels.'

Palmer laughed, a sour sound.

'You were done, my friend. I did her a favour, got you taken off the list. And what thanks did I get? You couldn't even do the job right!'

'I should have used the old, cold steel.'

Palmer was infuriated by the man's claim to soldier slang. If Lanier had ever seen cold steel, it was from a safe distance as far as he was concerned.

'Why let Shakespeare go – did *she* tell you to?'

'What? I don't know what you mean. Believe me, he was due to go too – my idea, shouldn't say, but he was.'

'You didn't want any witnesses?'

'More than that. Doesn't matter now, you're going to kill me anyway.'

Palmer tightened his hold on the man again to reinforce the impression.

'He was no threat to you, was he, *was he*,' Palmer shouted, grabbing Lanier's chin in an iron grip, threatening to slam his head into the wall again.

The man blew hard, struggling to clear his airways.

'Oh, but he was.'

'Why?'

'He knew more...'

'What about – *tell me*!'

'He saw me.'

'Saw you when?'

'No, saw me with ... saw me with...'

Palmer pulled his head back again. A stream of blood and mucus accompanied Lanier's words.

'... with the men who paid for the Richard play ... when we came to Bankside ... to fix it up.'

'At the Globe?'

'No, too obvious. There's an alehouse they use nearby, the actors...'

Palmer remembered it, where he had met Hemmings and Phillips.

'He was there when you...?'

'Yes, of course.'

Palmer let Lanier drop into the filthy gutter.

'You're slime, Lanier,' he said in disgust.

It was several hours before Palmer lurched back into his tenement chamber, half-lit by the taper he had wrenched from a boy paid to light his way home. He'd had a night of heavy drinking. A last call at the brothel in Turnmill Street nearby had failed to dispel his angry mood. It had also failed to excite his lust.

'Could do better'n this,' he struggled to say looking around in the swaying light and shadows.

There was no reason not to – he had the money.

A candle of ecclesiastical proportions appeared to move in and out of the reach of his taper. He steadied himself, planted both feet and supported his right arm with his left in an attempt to make contact between the taper and the candle.

The candle popped into flame, throwing a comforting glow around it.

'Shithole!' he mumbled, looking around at the sparse space, shabby in every particular except for the bed, his ark. He imagined its last bedmate.

'*Mrs* Lanier,' he laughed as he nearly tripped up into the bed's embrace. What was she doing now? Patching up her husband's busted face? He doubted it.

The memory of what he had done to the man briefly sobered him. Not so fucking useless as Lanier, do what I'm paid to do, not like fucking Lanier. Should have realised that Shakessssss...peare knew more than he was saying. Waddusitmatter. Got the money...

Worry sent an anxious hand rummaging inside his clothes. The purse was still there, and something else, a parcel, *the* parcel. He took it out then threw it on the bed where its shoddy packaging broke open.

He slumped down onto the bed. He pulled out a sheet at random and read it, twice over before the words began to mean much.

> '*Let me not to the marriage of true minds*
> *Admit impediments. Love is not love*
> *Which alters when it alteration finds.*'

The words swam. Palmer tried focusing with one eye. He skimmed a line opaque in meaning or impenetrable by his sodden mind. He read on.

> '*O no, it is an ever fixed mark*
> *That's looks on tempests and is never shaken.*'

It *was* shaken in the end. Palmer stifled a burp.

> '*Love alters not with his brief hours and weeks.*'

Brief hours and weeks.

> '*If this be error and upon me proved,*
> *I never writ and no man ever loved.*'

Palmer laughed at the fading black strokes dancing on parchment yellowed by candlelight.

He placed the sheet back in its place then he picked up the whole sheaf thrusting it close to the candle's flame, close enough for the corners to begin to curl. He thrust it forward a second time, and a third. It didn't catch. The wad was too tightly bound.

Better not, he hiccoughed, might set the bed on fire. He fell into it, rolled over and settled into a deep, dreamless sleep.

~ 17 ~

THE ROOM in the Tower was airless and oppressive. Candlelight illuminated the occupant's face which stared ahead, without expression, even when the visitors entered.

Southampton was sitting, listless, vaguely stroking a black cat which did not purr, used to dead men's hands. He looked ill, the skin pallid, his flesh already beginning to bloat through the effect of incarceration, lack of exercise and Government-ordered seclusion. He raised his eyes, appeared to recognise the first man in front of him and then returned to his cat-stroking. From the back of the room, Palmer saw that the once-confident mouth had fallen into despair.

The prisoner let out an irritable sigh, pushing the cat away. It slinked away in search of other prey.

Shakespeare sat down without speaking. Southampton glanced up again, a hint of anger in his dull eyes. With effort, he waved a hand around him as if in explanation or excuse. Then he fixed his visitors with an uncomfortable stare. The sound of his breathing accelerated. What are you doing here, his eyes seemed to accuse them?

'There is a way out of here,' Shakespeare began to say.

A muscle twitched at the corner of the prisoner's mouth triggering a hint of the once conquering smile. A flicker of his vanished charm flared for an instant. It disappeared just as quickly.

'There's nothing to be done,' Southampton interrupted him, his voice slurred. 'I did what I did, never mind why.'

'Think of your wife and family,' Shakespeare urged.

'I think you should listen to the offer,' Palmer added briskly from the back of the room.

He felt Southampton's eyes on him.

'Haven't we...?' the man began to ask.

Palmer shook his head, denying their shared sights of death and destruction in Essex House, the reek of gunpowder and the screams of dying men.

Quickly, Shakespeare explained Cecil's deal – the need for Essex to admit that he had intended to overthrow the Government and dispose of the Queen; the grant in return of a fitting execution and a platform on which Essex could expiate his conscience in public in front of his peers.

'Clever of Cecil, to appeal to Robert's conscience as well as his honour,' Southampton said, 'and I am to be the messenger? I see. And my *reward*?'

He pronounced the word with something like disdain. Survival was left unsaid but understood. He asked about his title, his lands and property.

Palmer shook his head.

'So,' Southampton rehearsed, his voice turning brisker, 'my life, such as it is, the name I was born with but not my title of nobility, no means to support myself or my family, and as for liberty – I stay locked away in the Tower.'

He looked around him.

'It's a lot to ask for so very little in return.'

'Your life,' Palmer reminded him.

'Such as it is or ever can be, world without end.'

Southampton laughed lightly at his own wit.

'Well, the Queen can't live forever, can she? *Can she?*'

Neither man replied.

'What makes you think my Lord Essex will listen to me?' Southampton challenged them.

Because you will make him, like you did before, Palmer reckoned quietly to himself. Their eyes met. Southampton's acknowledged him.

'Well, I will *try*,' he said.

He looked hard at Shakespeare.

'He will want some fine words, at the end, Will. A farewell speech, in your most *appealing* style.'

'Mr Shakespeare is to attend the execution,' Palmer said.

In one plan, Chief Minister Cecil was not so lucky. This was his idea for a command performance to keep the Queen's mind off Essex. It was deliberately set for the day before the execution. It was to be performed by the Lord Chamberlain, Hunsdon's Men, Shakespeare's acting company, in the Palace of Whitehall.

Her Highness was not at all happy.

The first Cecil knew about it was from the Master of the Revels, the court official responsible for royal entertainment. On Cecil's recommendation after consultation with Hunsdon, the Master had put forward the woodland romance which pleased the Queen at Christmas.

'HH doesn't like it,' Tilney's message said, this from a man who had dealt with her for a quarter of a century, 'but she will not say why. She wants to see you about it as soon as possible.'

Cecil decided to take Hunsdon with him as the sponsor of the acting company and one of her few close relatives. The Hunsdons and the Cecils, together Elizabeth's mainstays for over half a century...

'Well?' Elizabeth demanded when the two courtiers appeared before her.

Richly embroidered fabric in a fleur-de-lys pattern, pearls and a flame-coloured wig held up the tiny, feeble figure within and took attention away from the fine-lined, whitened face.

'If the play does not please Your Highness, it will be no trouble to withdraw it,' Cecil suggested.

'Just so,' Hunsdon chimed in. 'My actors only wish to please their Queen.'

'Pity they forgot that when the rebels asked for the Richard play!'

Both men knew better than to respond. They waited for their royal mistress's next words.

'So, As You Like It? Well, I *do not* like it!'

She offered no reason why.

'It will be no trouble, Highness, to cancel the performance,' Hunsdon was quick to repeat.

'No!'

'What would please Your Highness – another company, a different play?'

The voice was Cecil's. Elizabeth cocked her head.

'There *is* one play I have not seen...'

Neither man was quick enough to guess.

'... the Richard play!'

'Your Highness!'

Alarm exploded from both men at the same time.

'You ask me what I want and so I tell you! For God's sake, it has been performed on the stage, in private houses and in the streets for all I know, and by *your* company, Hunsdon. Well, now *I* shall see it.'

'Your Highness—' Hunsdon began to appeal once more.

'—has made a wise choice,' Cecil interrupted him, giving him to understand with a look of the eye that there was some advantage to be had. Perhaps it was time his mistress confronted the play for what it was, and was not...

'Yes,' the Queen said fiercely, 'let the actors do for me what they were only too willing to do for the rebels. Let us see what these *loyal* servants are made of.'

~ 18 ~

THE ACTORS in the alehouse appeared happy to be working again, once they got over their shock at the substance of the Queen's command. Shakespeare was taken aside by Palmer who had brought the order from the Chief Minister. Palmer's instructions were terse.

'There can't be any mistakes over this. The Chief Minister reckons that there is nothing to be afraid of. He says he's seen the play himself and he believes that if you and your colleagues do it justice then the meaning will be clear. The Queen will not take offence.'

'And she wants to see the play uncut?'

With the deposition scene in mind, was the writer just for once hoping for censorship, Palmer asked himself? If he was, it was not in the Chief Minister's orders.

'Entirely as you wrote it,' he insisted.

John Hemmings came over to them.

'I could be writing my death warrant,' Shakespeare said.

'We are all in this together, Will.'

Shakespeare was not reassured.

'No, John, I am the author, you and the others are the actors of my words.'

'Messengers often pay the price.'

Shakespeare fell silent.

'Then we have to put on a very good show!' Hemmings roared for all to hear, clapping his old colleague on the back, ignoring the investigator.

'One more thing,' Palmer said. 'I'm to be your minder – Chief Minister's orders.'

There was a lot to do in a little time.

The company set to work the day after in the Blackfriars Theatre where the Master of the Revels had authorised the actors to rehearse. It was an indoors playhouse on the north bank of the river, inside the City walls. The Globe syndicate owned its lease, only the authorities never let them act there – respectable locals had objected, Richard Field among them, Palmer called to mind as he passed awkward hours in the company of play and players. Now they had their chance.

Palmer watched Shakespeare standing on the stage, gazing into the auditorium out front. It was reckoned to be a useful model for the Great Chamber where the actors were required to perform in the Palace of Whitehall.

'The acoustic is very different from what we are used to in the open air at the Globe, Mr Palmer,' Shakespeare announced from the stage. 'Our actors will adjust easily enough. Most of us have performed at court before.'

'And you've already had the benefit of a run-through.'

It was not the most subtle statement by the investigator, referring to the performance put on to get the mob in the mood for regicide.

Shakespeare made no answer. Hemmings came over to join him.

'Three days to rehearse! Why my boy, it's positive luxury!'

Shakespeare called for the prompter. He upset the man by calling for the original text without the regular cuts.

'Means new play rolls for the actors,' the prompter grumbled.

'I want it done as I wrote it – for once,' Shakespeare said.

He gave instructions to Phillips about the music.

'We'll have the full consort of instruments.'

'Recorders and hautboys, viols, lute of course...'

'Wind and drums for the court scenes. Not too big a band though, we're not outdoors. We don't want to deafen our audience.'

Phillips understood.

Shakespeare called his King Richard over.

'You want me to be careful not to overplay it,' Dick Burbage said to Shakespeare, eyeing Palmer with distrust.

The playwright put his arm round the actor.

'All I ask is this. Richard remains no less a king despite what happens to him. His character is sacred right to the end. Remember that in the final prison scene – dignified as well as pathetic.'

'You didn't ask me over just to tell me that, Will.'

Shakespeare laughed, gently for once.

'No, I didn't. It's about our Bolingbroke the usurper.'

'Very experienced, Will, even if what you see is what you get.'

'I do, Dick, but this is not the Globe and shouting over all that rabble and noise. I was thinking of somebody else.'

'Who?'

'Our Fortinbras in the Danish play.'

From the auditorium Palmer saw a strange look appear on Burbage's face.

'Your brother Edmund? It's such a gamble, Will.'

'It is but he's young, as young as...'

...Essex in his prime, Palmer asked himself? Or Southampton in their sonnet spring?

~ 19 ~

IT WAS A SHORT TIME before the performance in Whitehall.

Palmer followed Shakespeare into the actors' makeshift dressing space. The playwright had decided not to appear in the play; it made matters easier in shifting the parts round in order to introduce his brother Edmund as Bolingbroke. He was instead to take up his position at the side of the stage among the musicians from where, he explained, he could keep an eye on proceedings.

The odour of actors' bodies assaulted Palmer's nose – sweat and unwashed feet mixed with the damp mustiness of costumes brought out of store. Polished leather and brightly-scoured metal interjected sharper smells of the muster ground which the old soldier in Palmer recognised.

He watched the actors go about their pre-performance routines – the gossipers whose brains switched on only when they were called; the silent solitaries, checking their lines from their rolls – openly or furtively; the fiddlers with their costumes and the nervous throat clearers.

Shakespeare was looking for his brother Edmund. He soon found him, one of the silent solitaries in the corner. The boy looked pale to Palmer's eyes from his safe distance. For the lad to learn a new part was one thing, he guessed, but to go out onstage in front of an unpredictable hive at the heart of which was the queen bee herself, it was bound to be a tall order.

He watched Shakespeare go over to his brother.

'How are you feeling?' the older brother asked.

Edmund gulped an unconvincing reply. Shakespeare reassured him.

'You've done the work, you were good in rehearsals. I'm glad we've put you in the part. Now, remember what I've taught you.'

'Speak the words naturally, no shouting, don't overdo the gestures.'

'Suit the actions to the words...'

'... and the words to the actions!' the two men chanted in unison before breaking into their strange, explosive family laugh.

Palmer saw Hemmings smile.

'The laugh's back!' the actor announced to everyone.

'Time to start the music?' Phillips asked.

Shakespeare gave the sign.

As he went out front through a side door, Palmer ducked in behind him. They arrived at the side of the stage, to soft sounds of woodwind and strings grounded by a bass viol.

The Great Chamber was not especially long – maybe sixty feet deep, Palmer estimated looking round him, half that in width, all under a high ceiling. Tapestried walls and candlelit illumination completed the rich effect as well as cosseting the musical sounds.

A sudden flurry at the entrance caught his eye. It announced the arrival of the Queen.

'Just her immediate followers,' Palmer whispered to Shakespeare, from what he had been told by the chief official to the Chief Minister.

The facing cast took their places – Elizabeth, doll-like and glittering, perched on a gilded chair set part of the way down the room; Cecil's tiny figure was almost lost in the grouping, giving ground to Hunsdon who was doing what he did best on such occasions, talking affably to his sovereign and kinswoman; this trio set against a smattering of courtiers behind them.

'They look a grim bunch,' Palmer whispered, eyes out front.

'We're lions in a den of Daniels,' Shakespeare said, stifling his nervous laugh.

The Master of the Revels waved for the play to begin in a pompous show of his authority. Two trumpeters stood up, wooden cornets at the ready. The senior player gave a nod of his head, launching the pair into a crisp fanfare. The stage filled up busily with actor-bodies summoned by the clarion calls, drawing all eyes to it including Palmer's.

The regal voice of Richard rang out.

'Old John of Gaunt, time-honoured Lancaster,
Hast thou according to thy oath and bond
Brought hither Henry Bolingbroke, thy bold son.'

Burbage was straight into his stride. Even to Palmer, each word struck clearly in the actor's flexible tenor voice. Richard's throne was addressing Elizabeth's, from gilded chair to chair.

The young Bolingbroke in contrast started nervously, stumbling on his opening words.

Suddenly the illusion was suspended, ready to break and fall into pieces. Palmer sensed Shakespeare tense beside him. Was nobody going to give the lad the line?

The actor found it for himself, and his rhythm and with it the character.

Palmer heard his brother breathe again.

A noisy vocal battle broke out unchecked between the quarrelling lords, Bolingbroke and Norfolk, accusations of treason, fraud and the murder of royal blood until King Richard overrode them. He called for trial by combat.

'Shifty lot, those Norfolks,' the Queen was heard to say. She had executed a Norfolk in her time for plotting against her. Cecil appeared to nod sagely at her wisdom.

Cornets sounded, summoning both noble rivals. Proper armour, metal strapped with leather, its burnish gleaming brightly in the soft candlelight, made the scene real in look and smell.

Noble counterblasted noble.

'Men's quarrels don't change,' the Queen announced to those around her who duly smiled.

A cornet call signalled for the combat to begin.

'Stay! The King hath thrown his warder down.'

King Richard stepped down from his throne to where his gauntlet lay between the two combatants. Queen Elizabeth leaned forward from hers, interested in what the King would pronounce – banishment abroad for both men was what she heard. Elizabeth fell back, a slight, sharp movement, unconvinced.

A sad parting between Bolingbroke and his father John of Gaunt, uncle to the King, took over the stage. Their feelings interwove deftly, like phrases between answering instruments until Bolingbroke exited the stage with a flourish.

'Wher'er I wander, boast of this I can:
Though banished, yet a trueborn Englishman!'

It went unrewarded by applause.

'His rash fierce blaze of riot cannot last,
For violent fires soon burn out themselves.'

Hemmings's delivery as the now-dying Gaunt rumbled over and around the room. His words grew more and more sleep-inducing to Palmer.

'… royal throne … scepter'd isle … precious stone … something something … silver sea … this realm, this … *England!'*

Still no applause.

Hemmings left the stage with too much flourish for a dying man.

'Very slow out front tonight,' he grumbled as he passed the band, going off.

Onstage King Richard gave orders for the confiscation of dead Gaunt's property for his own royal use. Palmer did not need to be told – it was Bolingbroke's inheritance and his ground for complaint against the King his cousin, a turning point in their fortunes?

'Unwise, unwise,' the Queen murmured in her stage whisper.

Which was pretty rich, Palmer reckoned given her own record of fines and dispossessions including his own family estate in Kent.

As if to prove her right, a clutch of stage nobles clustered in conspiracy, to bring back Bolingbroke to England to right his wrongs. Military scenes hurried by, piling up to create the effect of impending war. Sackbuts and drums joined the cornets to flavour the martial mood.

Palmer's veteran eye at first despised the onstage business. It was a parody of the real thing yet, he was forced to concede, in the constant movement, colour and noise and the marching and countermarching of a few bodies in organised confusion, something of the atmosphere of battle ebbed and flowed in front of him.

It was enough to bring King Richard low. The King bewailed his fate.

> *'What must the King do now? Must he submit?*
> *The King shall do it. Must he be......* deposed?'

The terrible word! It dropped from Burbage's mouth, hanging in the air.

Palmer saw Elizabeth grasp the arms of her throne. Life inside the chamber froze. Richard had no answer to his own question, until the words came out as if shaken from him.

'… the King shall be contented.'

He crumbled into humility.

'And my large kingdom for a little grave,
A little grave, an obscure grave…'

'Stop!'

A voice held up the drama on the stage. It held unique authority. It was the Queen's.

The mood in the dressing room was heavily subdued when Shakespeare went back into it, closely followed by Palmer.

Hemmings was full of apology.

'Dear boy, I'm sorry if I overdid it.'

A movement behind him cut him short. Standing in the doorway was the Master of the Revels, Tilney. The look on his face gave the actors no grounds for optimism. The room fell silent.

'Shakespeare? Come with me!'

'*Mr* Shakespeare!' an anonymous voice protested from among the actors, without much conviction.

Shakespeare went, followed by his shadow.

'Chief Minister's orders – where he goes, I go,' Palmer said when challenged.

They found the Queen waiting for them on her throne chair in the chamber. She had dismissed her privy councillors, all

except Cecil and Hunsdon who were hovering in the
background.

'Come here!'

The command came from the Queen. It did not sound
kind.

Palmer watched Shakespeare approach the throne, head
lowered. The Queen did not extend her hand to be kissed –
another bad sign.

'So that was your Richard play.'

Past tense. Ominous, Palmer reckoned.

'You presume to describe, no, to put on public *exhibition*
the deposition of a crowned king anointed by God?'

Shakespeare made no answer.

'I imagine that you were about to tack on, for public
entertainment, his wicked, sacrilegious murder. That *is* the
scene which follows? Answer me!'

'Your Highness, the scene which follows is the palace
gardeners.'

'Ah! The gardeners, those great men of state!' Her call over
her shoulder towards Cecil and Hunsdon brought knowing
smiles in return. 'What do they know, those *grass roots*!'

'The gardener is who I usually play, Your Highness,'
Shakespeare said.

And so? the silence seemed to say.

Shakespeare spoke again.

'May I give one small part of it?'

The Master of the Revels stepped smartly forward to
restrain him but the Queen waved the official back. She
completed the movement of her hand, bringing it down and
turning it over. It was license to Shakespeare to proceed.

He cleared his throat. His mind appeared to search for the
opening line.

  '*O, what pity it is*......

O, what a pity it is
That he – the King – had not so trimm'd and dressed his land
As we this garden.'

Shakespeare stopped, as if searching for more.
'Is that all?' the Queen demanded.
The actor's voice started up again.

'*We........at this time of year*
Do wound the bark, the skin of our fruit trees,
Lest........being over-proud in sap......and blood
With too much riches it confound itself.'

The chamber's political temperature fell several degrees further. Curbing the over-mighty, Palmer wondered, was that wise to suggest? All eyes turned to the Queen.

'I would expect a gardener to say that,' she pronounced, 'plants are all they care for. But I must care for my subjects whether they want it or not. Well, go on.'

Shakespeare obeyed.

'*Had he – the King – done so to great and growing men,*
They might have lived to bear, and he to taste
Their fruits of duty.'

Not what he would have chosen, Palmer told himself – it was a terrible risk to remind a sovereign of her responsibility. How high the royal temper would blow appeared to be the only question on all the strained faces he saw in the room.

The Queen settled back in her seat.

'And is that what you believe?'

'It is what the gardener believes, Your Highness. It's a wise soul who listens to his gardener.'

The Queen raised a fan to her face. She lowered it gently. She was smiling.

'Remarkable,' she said.

She turned to her two privy councillors.

'He examines men's thoughts but he does not judge them. I thought all plays existed to point a moral but he tells me otherwise.'

Then she smiled again. Cecil and Hunsdon joined in with her, warming the atmosphere around the room.

'Come nearer,' the Queen commanded Shakespeare.

She motioned him to sit at her feet.

Queen spoke to actor.

'We have not been the best of friends you and I ... oh, I *have* loved your plays! But you came too late, you found me past my glory – there were others more fertile for your skills. No matter,' she said, resisting his protest. 'Monarchs can have no friends, not if they are to rule wisely.'

Elizabeth turned her head away, towards Cecil.

'No word from my Lord Essex?'

Cecil shook his head.

'Some plants resist even their gardener's care,' she said sadly then turned her eyes back towards the man still seated in front of her. 'Mr Shakespeare, I am sorry I stopped your play. It was meant to divert a queen from her concerns, but, as you see, it could not help the woman beneath the crown.'

~ 20 ~

THE SCARLET WAISTCOAT Essex revealed when he stripped off his black cloak and doublet provoked a shiver of shock among the witnesses in the Tower courtyard present for his execution. The theatrical choice conveying blood and sacrifice was not lost on the onlookers.

'The warrant's been going back and forth like nobody's business,' Cecil's chief official had confided to Palmer as he made the arrangements for the investigator and the author to attend. The Queen had baulked at signing it, he gave him to understand.

'He looks like the phoenix,' Palmer heard Shakespeare say, standing next to him while a cold winter wind whistled round them, whipped up off the river outside the Tower walls. So Essex was matching red with red for when the blow fell from the executioner's blade. It was the colour of martyrdom. Palmer understood what was going on – a legend was being created. Cecil could not control everything. A man's impending death gave him inalienable privilege.

It was Ash Wednesday at dawn, the beginning of the season of penitence. The coincidence was intended, Palmer had no doubt. He watched Essex struggle to undo his collar, movement enough to keep the man's hands from shaking. Job done, Essex turned to face the onlookers. He launched into a dignified plea for forgiveness for what he had done.

'... for this great, this bloody, this crying and this infectious sin.'

Prayerbook-sounding stuff, Palmer thought. He turned to look at Shakespeare, saw his lips moving in rhythm with Essex's words – his 'appealing words' as Southampton had sardonically suggested when the deal was proposed in the dank, lightless cell. There was no Southampton present to hear them. He was locked sight- and sound-lessly away elsewhere in the Tower.

Essex was struggling to be heard over the unsympathising wind. Palmer strained to hear what he was confessing.

'... my sin through which so many, for love of me, have risked their lives and souls, and have been induced to offend God, to offend their Sovereign and to offend the world.'

Not a trivial charge-sheet, Palmer reckoned.

The Earl's voice rose higher still in combat with the wind.

'So I desire all the world to forgive me, even as I, freely and from my heart, forgive the world.'

He kneeled down to pray.

'Our Father, which art in Heaven...'

Palmer mouthed the words silently out of ancient habit and saw Shakespeare doing the same. A few gruff voices sounded them aloud.

After the Amen, Essex knelt forward. He put his head on the block in front of him. The executioner made ready to strike.

Out of the corner of his eye Palmer saw Shakespeare look away. Palmer didn't care for executions either. It was not the sight of death – he had seen far worse, far uglier in war – it was the reaction of the onlookers; animal satisfaction for the most part was what he was expecting.

The executioner looked nervous. Palmer watched the heavy blade rise unsurely, reflecting the oyster colour of the morning light. It bobbed for an instant at its apex, and fell.

A tortured yelp.

Not dead then, Palmer knew at once; the executioner had missed his aim.

The panicked headsman wrenched the blade free from the shoulder of the condemned man. The body lay slumped and motionless. Essex had fainted, Palmer could see – thank Christ for that.

'The man's passed out,' he whispered to Shakespeare, 'he's beyond it now.'

The executioner's second strike fell off target as well, into an inert body which gave up a dull, sucking thud. Sweating, the headsman wound himself up for a third attempt.

This time, the head, or what was left of it, rolled clear.

It began a season of executions.

Palmer and Shakespeare were sent to watch when Essex's steward and his secretary were hanged in front of the mob at Tyburn in the west, cut down alive, disembowelled and their hearts ripped out before their fading sight.

The dead bodies were expertly cut into quarters for public display.

'Strung up, then gutted like animals on the butcher's slab.'

Palmer could not disagree with the writer's bitter epitaph.

It was back east for the execution of Essex's old tooth-shattered stepfather, for more confessions and a surer fall of the blade this time, in sight of a holiday crowd on Tower Hill.

'The remaining ringleaders will pay a fortune in fines,' the chief official told Palmer, repeating what he had heard from his master.

It was a price worth paying, Palmer imagined, for those with the money and the determination to hang on for better times. The great She, she could not last forever.

'Southampton?' he had asked the official.

Southampton was to stay shut away in limbo in the Tower.

When the State's amusements were concluded, the places of public entertainment reopened.

Palmer crossed the river to the Globe on Bankside in order to deliver one final message for his client the Chief Minister. He paid his extra threepence to enter the galleries, looking over a standing audience which steamed and stank under sunny spring skies mixed with showers.

The play in front of him was a woodland romance, the success of the year before. It made sense, he guessed – lighter fare for folk out of sorts with anything more serious after recent events.

He recognised old acquaintances among the actors onstage. Edmund Shakespeare bounded up and down as a lovesick swain packed full of bad poetry in praise of a boy playing girl playing boy. Palmer caught echoes of the sonnets he had, somewhere, stored away in his chamber. What should he do with them now?

His train of thought was interrupted by Hemmings booming away below him as an exiled duke. When an old retainer struggled on, sacrificing himself for a younger man, it came as no surprise to Palmer who was playing the part – Shakespeare. Where had he heard that one before? And how had it turned out when the sacrifice was called on in real life? People rarely lived up to their ideals, only his holy father – and see what that had achieved!

Not that any of it mattered now. Once this last task was completed, there was no further business to do for Cecil. The agent's own usefulness was over, at least for the time being. The money made would buy time. What then?

The play closed to the applause which a witty epilogue by the boy-girl-boy demanded, giving way to a company jig of bawdy song and dance. It intrigued Palmer just how nimbly Shakespeare moved. Wasn't he meant to have played an old man?

Afterwards he found the actors where he expected, in their favourite alehouse.

'You're not welcome here,' Phillips said, sent over to confront him.

'Just tell Old Adam over there that I have a last message for him – from the Chief Minister.'

Phillips retreated. Palmer watched him gesticulating among his colleagues who looked back across at him with coldness and suspicion.

Shakespeare emerged from the group and came towards him. Under the smart town clothes the man looked harder, tempered in the refiner's fire. He stopped short, waiting for the message and nothing more.

'What are you working on now?' Palmer asked, drawing the moment out, repeating the convention he had heard among actors.

'You have not come here to ask me that. What is it you have to tell me?'

'Southampton will live – but pardon isn't in the deal. Don't expect to see him, not while the Queen's alive. They're sending the official scavengers down to Southampton's estate. They'll confiscate what's there.'

Palmer had his own family memories of daylight robbery by the State.

'Here's to better times,' Shakespeare said, 'and soon.'

Palmer raised an eyebrow.

'What happened to the reconciliation in the Great Chamber?' he asked.

'Foreclosed by the rope and the axe.'

Palmer shrugged – the authorities had been moderate under the circumstances. Wasn't Southampton alive?

'So, I'm free of you at last, Mr Palmer,' Shakespeare said.

'Depends if you stay out of trouble.'

'And you think I won't?'

Palmer chose his moment.

'Look, I know what really happened. Lanier told me – I beat it out of him.'

'You believe Lanier?'

'You could deny Southampton nothing.'

'I wasn't at the Globe when the arrangement was made.'

'That, Mr Shakespeare, is playing with words.'

'Words are my business.'

'You were lucky this time,' Palmer said, 'words can be dangerous things.'

A line came into his mind –

'From fairest creatures we desire increase.'

He repeated them out loud.

'From a sonnet, by William Shakespeare,' he said.

'He wrote better ones.'

'Good enough to last?'

'There was once a poet used to think so.'

Both men looked at each other in silence before Shakespeare turned away to rejoin his friends.

Palmer watched him go then walked towards the open door. As he passed through it, the noise in the room picked up.

~ Closing the File ~

'They say our new King James, 'e's at Berwick, wherever that is.'

The landlord of the Bell in Carter Lane threw an enquiring glance to Richard Palmer whose tick had not been paid for some time. It was two years since he had seen his customer flush with cash.

'On the border with Scotland,' Palmer answered without enthusiasm.

'Bound to be changes,' the landlord speculated. 'What's it mean for us all, Dick?'

What indeed? Nothing much for the common folk, Palmer reckoned without saying it, taxes as before, not fewer, likely more. But for the big folk, now that was different.

Take Southampton. He'd heard it from the Chief Minister's chief official, a continuing source of gossip but no money – Southampton was to be released from the Tower and reinstated. Scots King James liked a handsome face and a gallant leg, it was said. A Knight of the Garter Southampton was to be and high in the court of the new Queen, a subtle move. Patience rewarded? More like stay alive and your turn will come again. It was a lesson he was holding onto himself.

And Cecil? From knight to high nobility, increased title and power. James was nothing if not even-handed with his largesse. Onetime accuser and accused were to rub shoulders together in worship of the new royal sun and moon.

It was prizes all round. Survivors in the Essex crew now had their snouts firmly in the trough. The Essex son and heir was to receive marks of royal favour in honour of the 'martyrdom' of his father. Palmer had even heard that Lanier was putting

himself in line for some perk or other. MacLanier the pisspot of
that ilk! Maybe it would please his wife Emilia, for her bastard
brat.

'What about that actor feller you was chasin' after?' the
landlord asked.

Oh yes, Shakespeare. The plays kept on tumbling out, not
that Palmer made any effort to see them, not even the Trojan
one the playwright had sketched out for him on the ride back
from Stratford. Field, whom he'd seen just once by chance,
prospering and rising in the Stationers Company, told him it
was too cynical even for the London stage; it had quietly been
put aside after a run out in the universities. 'His plays of late
are dark, very dark,' the printer confided. Not as dark as an
unfee'd, unfed investigator, Palmer had grumbled at the time.

And now the greatest irony of all – the new King and
Queen so adored the drama that each was to sponsor a
company of actors, their children likewise. London was going
to be crawling with the thespian vermin! William Shakespeare?
He was to be one of the King's Men, generously transferred by
Lord Chamberlain Hunsdon to his royal master. Now there
was a man who knew how to make a gift before it was extracted
from him!

'He'll walk in the procession at the coronation in the King's
livery,' the chief official, who was excited by such things, had
told Palmer along with the colour, cut and quality of the cloth
the actor would be entitled to.

Palmer, whose suit was now getting as old and as shabby as
its predecessor could barely bring himself to listen. It might
mean something for Shakespeare's daughter Susanna and her
prospects, whatever they might be. He surprised himself by
hoping that it would. She at least deserved to come out well
from this upside down world.

So what about me, Palmer wondered but refused to ask even when the chief official prattled on about a new era of unity, peace and prosperity, a golden age which was to have no evident use for informers and investigators. Christ! the man even had hopes for the toleration of the old faith, what with a philosopher king on the throne and his consort rumoured to have Catholic proclivities. Was this friend of his father-the-holy-fool looking forward to coming out, from behind the arras of a lifetime's religious masquerade?

At least the old Alderman came back to Palmer from time to time about his flighty young wife, frequently enough for him to realise that what the man liked most were salacious details, so he laid them on thick in his reports. It gave the man more pleasure than he shared with his wife in bed. The income kept Palmer alive, just, that and the tick he got at the Bell.

'Yes, what's it mean for us all?' the landlord repeated.

'Another dose of the plague, that's the only safe bet in this world,' Palmer replied, gazing into his empty mug.

This promised golden age, it needed upsetting...

Lightning Source UK Ltd.
Milton Keynes UK
UKOW04f1901121115

262627UK00001B/25/P